MW00638096

Thrive

Allow Jesus to move you from ordinary to extraordinary in every area of your life.

By: Timothy Jemly

Dedication

For my Lord and Savior Jesus Christ who's made it possible for me to both thrive in this life and to live forever with Him. I owe you my life and every aspect of who I am. And for my wife, Amber and my daughter, Lucia who bring such joy and richness to my life. Thank you both for your love and unwavering loyalty.

Contents

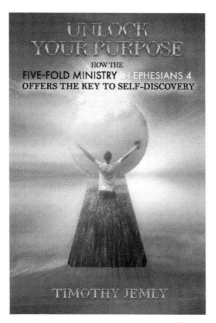

Free Book

Part of thriving is knowing and living out your purpose. I have included a chapter in this book on discovering your purpose. But if you'd like to go deeper I'm offering a free ecopy of my book "Unlock your Purpose." Please visit https://timothyjemly.com/freebook to claim yours today.

Introduction

I came across a news story recently about a poor couple who won a 7-day cruise in the Caribbean. They were really excited about the opportunity to go to fresh places and see things they hadn't experienced before. They'd never been on a cruise and had little money, so they packed crackers, cheese and other snacks to live on for the week. Every day they saw people dressed up and going out to dinner, but they stayed in their cabin and ate their crackers and cheese. On the last day of the cruise, they discovered their tickets included all the food! They could eat at any restaurant on the ship, whatever they wanted for no cost.

Some people have a similar experience with life. Many have the mistaken notion that God only cares about their ultimate destination. They look forward to being in heaven someday, but don't realize there are many blessing available now. I'm not talking about a name it and claim it theology where life is all lollipops and roses. Our world is broken and as long as we live here, we'll have trouble. However, God has a plan for you to thrive regardless of your circumstances. There are blessings available to you right now; you just need to know how to access them.

When I was growing up, my family moved around a lot. I learned to make friends quickly and easily, but not to hold on to them too tightly. I had a close relationship with my immediate family, but otherwise deep relationships were scarce. School always came easy to me. I got straight A's, but I never had to strive for them. My family always seemed to struggle financially, but we had what we needed. In high school, I was confident and ready to make my mark on the world. Then my mom passed away during my senior year.

When she died, it drove me closer to God, but it also made me consider how brief life is and what I wanted out of it. Jesus said He came that we might have life and have it more abundantly. I didn't believe He was only referring to our future in heaven, yet as I looked around it didn't seem like most of the Christians were thriving. I decided to whole-heartedly follow God and discover what the abundant life is all about.

A year later, I found myself at a college five hundred miles away from home. I had no close friends, and for the first time in my life I was struggling academically. I kept my A average, but only by spending all my free time studying. I had no social life; I didn't even have time to play the sports I enjoy. I was lonely, and my quest to find the abundant life seemed derailed.

I spent the next year as a missionary on a small island in the Pacific. That season helped me to reconnect not only with God but also with my purpose. I came back re-energized and inspired to lead young people into a deeper relationship with God. Having a purpose rekindled my enjoyment of every part of life.

Fast forward four years... I'm engaged to be married, I'm youth pastoring at a church in Oregon, and I'm really enjoying life. Then my boss told me he didn't think I'm cut out for ministry. I lost my job and my sponsorship to seminary. Suddenly, the purpose that had rekindled my life was cut out from under me.

Through the Spirit's guidance and much trial and error, I have found a place of abundance. Today I understand why I struggled so mightily, and I've learned how to access the abundant life Jesus died for me to have. I've realized It's possible to thrive amid **any** circumstance. I want to save others the heart ache and struggles I went through and help them thrive today.

I wrote this book because I know so many people who're merely surviving. They feel they're always on the outside with no place to belong. They believe everyone else has figured out a secret for success they just can't seem to grasp. I have so many friends who feel like they just don't measure up. They earn enough money to get by; they enjoy time with their families, and have fun on the weekends, but have no passion or enthusiasm for life. Others seem to be living in the future, they're driven and desire a better future than they're currently enjoying, but the future never seems to arrive. A few people excel and seem to thrive in certain areas, but when you look closer, you discover their life is a train wreck in other areas. We need to thrive in five different spheres. If we can't thrive in one of them, it will poison the other areas and we will fail to thrive altogether.

For example, I know a guy—let's call him Rick—who worked his tail off and became wealthy. Rick owns several large homes, boats, cars and even a private plane. His motto is "work hard and play harder" ~ and he does. He also works out regularly and has an enviable physique. Rick has a life many people try to emulate, but they don't realize he has basically no relationship with his kids and his wife is on the verge of filing for divorce. He feels guilty and shameful that he doesn't spend more time with his family, but the few encounters he has with them always seem to end in anger and resentment. Rick doesn't want to deal with those negative emotions; so he throws himself into more work. He has also started drinking heavily, even when he isn't partying. Rick knows his situation isn't healthy, but he's powerless to change anything.

I need to be upfront and inform you I am writing from a faith-based perspective. This doesn't mean you have to be Christian or even a person of faith to benefit from this book. Many of the principles I teach will work for you regardless of your belief system, but I need your permission to be who I am and to speak from my experience. I draw the principles I am teaching from scripture and quote it throughout.

If you aren't a believer, I hope this won't make you uncomfortable. Please know that I don't judge or condemn. Please also understand that while many of these simple steps will work even if you aren't a Christian, one can't fully enjoy the abundant life God desires for us without a relationship with Him. I won't belittle anyone or try to force my belief system on you, but I feel the need to be up front about this.   The simple principles I am talking about are universal and can help you achieve greatness in every area of your life, but those principles came from God and are used most effectively with His guidance.

In this introduction I am explaining the theoretical framework for why the simple steps in this book work. I am doing this for my readers who like to ask "Why". If this isn't you, feel free to skip to chapter one and begin learning the practical steps you can take today to go from merely surviving to thriving. However, if you're a person who likes to understand the "why" and you enjoy a little theory, then read on.

The five vital spheres we all need to thrive in are finances, relationships, health, emotions, and spirituality.

In this book, I teach the practical steps needed to thrive in each area. God created the universe in such a way that everything functions according to established rules and patterns. If you learn to live your life in alignment with these principles, then you will thrive in that area.

Let me give you a concrete example to help you understand what I am talking about. Gravity is one of the basic laws governing the universe. Over two years ago, I was rock climbing and forgot to clip in. I fell about 25 feet and shattered my hip, fractured my left arm and broke some ribs. The moment I fell gravity wasn't my friend, but I have never blamed gravity for my fall. Gravity is a good law, and it's an excellent design by the Maker of the universe. The problem isn't gravity; the problem was, I wasn't living my life in alignment with the law of gravity. When I fly on an airplane, I'm still in alignment with the law of gravity. An airplane doesn't defy gravity. No, it utilizes other physical laws that allow it to overcome gravity. The more we understand all the laws of physics, the more we'll able to use them to accomplish what we desire.

In the same way, there are moral and spiritual laws governing our universe. These aren't arbitrary rules with an authoritarian God trying to enforce them. They're "design laws" telling us how we can thrive as human beings. When I buy a new car, it comes with an owner's manual, which tells what I need to do to maintain the car. Imagine if I got upset that they were expecting me to maintain the vehicle and refused to bring my car in for maintenance. What if I decided their rules were ridiculous, and I wouldn't follow them? If I ignore the owner's manual and don't perform any of the scheduled maintenance or even change the oil, what will happen to my car? I'll end up trashing my engine. If that were to happen, I'd be crazy to blame the car or the manufacturer for my problems. But many people blame their circumstances or God for the problems in their life when, in fact, most of their problems result from their actions being out of alignment with the rules governing the universe.

Please note that I said MOST— not all of our problems. We live in a world out of sync with the laws governing it, so bad things happen to people through no fault of their own. However, it's always possible to thrive regardless of what our circumstances are because what happens TO us isn't nearly as important as what happens IN us. We don't have control of our circumstances, but we do have control over how we respond.

In John 10:10 Jesus said,

"The thief's purpose is to steal and kill and destroy. My purpose is to give them a rich and satisfying life." (NLT)

A rich and satisfying life sounds good to me; but sometimes my life has seemed dreary, bleak and unsatisfying. Those times left me wondering whether

Jesus had fulfilled His mission, or if the abundant life is something we won't experience until the next life. Eventually, I realized the problem: I was allowing the thief to steal and kill the things God was trying to bless me with!

The truth I've discovered on this journey is that God designed all of us to thrive in every area of our life. Sadly, God's design has gotten seriously messed up. As a Christian, I believe Jesus died to restore what I lost. Regrettably, most people still live in darkness and discouragement, because they have fallen for lies. I want to teach you how to confront those lies and step into the fullness of what He has for you. In this book, I will share with you the secrets I have learned for seeing the truth and releasing the good things God has stored up for you.

The things I am going to share won't magically transform your circumstances. Instead, they will transform you, and as you continue to learn and grow in your ability to live according to God's design, your circumstances will change as well. You can enjoy true abundance in your spirituality, emotional life, health, relationships, career, and finances by following the simple steps outlined in this book.

The basic premise I am building on is that God's instructions and laws aren't arbitrary. Some people have the notion that if you follow God's rules then He will bless you, and if you don't follow His rules perfectly then He will curse you. Many Christians also believe this, with the added caveat that because of Jesus' sacrifice, we can obtain grace so we get the blessings He deserved while Jesus took the curses which should have come on us. It's true that because of Jesus' sacrifice we can receive the blessings of God and are free from the penalty of sin, but the underlying assumption that the penalty is something God imposes because He's angry at us for breaking His law is out of line with what the Bible teaches about God. The Bible says God is love, but as atheists love to point out, a

God who will punish someone for eternity because they refused to obey Him doesn't seem very loving.

Consider this, we're created in the image of God—who's love. The Bible says love is the fulfillment of the law. Romans 13:10 says,

> "*Love does no harm to a neighbor. Therefore love is the fulfillment of the law." (NIV)*

Before sin entered the world, we didn't need the law; because God created us in His image, love came naturally for us. Sin is like a virus that has corrupted our operating system and made us incapable of loving as God does. Worse, it cuts us off from God who's the source of life. The Bible not only says God is love but also says He's light. 1 John 1:5 states,

> "*This is the message we have heard from him and declare to you: God is light; in him there is no darkness at all." (NIV)*

This virus not only made us incapable of loving perfectly as God does, it also linked humanity's soul with darkness. When light is introduced to darkness, it instantly destroys the darkness. Before sin corrupted us, Adam and Eve used to walk and talk with God face to face. Once sin corrupted the race, we could no longer exist in the presence of pure light—it would destroy us! Even the great Moses was told he couldn't see God's face and live. Not that God doesn't want us to look at Him. He's **not** saying, "*I will fry you if you dare to so much as glance at my face.*" Instead, He's simply stating a fact about our situation. Without an anti-virus, we're all doomed. We can't survive in God's presence and without a connection to Him we're all dying from the moment we're born because sin cut us off from the one who's the source of life.

To summarize, God designed the universe to operate on a set of physical, spiritual, and moral laws.

When we live our lives in alignment with these laws, good things result because we're operating in the way we're designed to. When we live our lives in opposition to these laws, bad things will happen because we're attempting to operate in a way the universe is not designed for. Sometimes bad things will happen to us even if we're operating inside the laws governing the universe because we live in a world that's ignoring many of those rules. When this happens, we can mitigate those negative effects if we continue to apply the principles I offer in this book. Hopefully, I've answered your "why's" and we can dive into the book together as I share "how".

Chapter One

The Big Secret

My wife and I once found ourselves stuck in a car that wouldn't start in a terrible neighborhood in East LA at 2 a.m. The police came by and told us, *"It isn't safe for you to be here—you need to leave."* I explained I would love to, but my car wouldn't start. They reiterated it wasn't safe and drove off. I called AAA, and they said it would take 6 hours for them to get there. Now, this was my brother's car, and he had warned me that sometimes when the steering wheel locks you have to jiggle it and hold in just the right position or the key won't turn. I kept doing what he had told me, but no matter what I tried, I couldn't get the key to turn. I had been trying for almost an hour when my wife said, *"Are you sure you're using the right key?"* I wasn't sure so I tried some others, and when I found the right one the key turned easily and the car started right up.

Like my brother's car, in your life there's a key that will make what's not been working suddenly work smoothy and easily. In the introduction to this book, I argued that God's law isn't a list of arbitrary rules, but it's a description of how things operate. When we live our lives in alignment with those spiritual laws we will flourish, just as we do when we live in alignment with the physical laws, such as gravity, that He created. This knowledge is about as useful as a screen door on submarine if you find you can't follow the guidelines. Many times, our failures aren't a result of not knowing what's right, but of our inability to do it. If your exercise routine involves banging your head against a wall, trying to figure out why you keep doing things you know you shouldn't do, this chapter is for you.

This amazing secret for transforming your life is called supersedimentarypremonitionalism, which not only is longer than almost any other word in the dictionary, but the concept it represents is the most incredible, amazing, awe-inspiring, incomprehensible thing in the universe. It will completely transform your life and change your way of seeing the world. It's incomparable to anything else you've ever heard or experienced.

That's great — you say, but what is supersedimentarypremonitionalism and do I have to pronounce it? It's very hard to define. It isn't like anything else, and there are no words that come close to capturing the full meaning of this word. There are some words that come close to capturing one aspect or another of it, but it's multi-faceted. It would require hundreds of words to capture all the unique aspects of this word, and nothing comes close to defining it. There is no sentence I could give you that would allow you to understand the true depths of this word. They say a story is worth a thousand words, so some might suggest perhaps there is a story that would capture the fullness of this word. There are in fact thousands of stories that demonstrate different aspects of supersedimentarypremonitionalism and I will share some of them, but I am afraid they still won't crystalize what this amazing, transformational concept is.

Thankfully, there's someone I know who perfectly embodies this concept. The easiest thing is to point to Him as an example of what I'm talking about. That person is Jesus. I have a confession to make: you won't find supersedimentarypremonitionalism in any dictionary because I made up the word—but not the concept. The idea it represents is **grace.** I made up the word because most people think they know what grace is. Nearly everyone has experienced and understands at least some aspects of grace. But there's much more to grace than we've commonly understood. It is diamond we will turn and study for all of eternity, seeking fully to understand its depths.

When we hear the word 'grace' we sometimes think it just means 'unmerited favor' or 'letting someone off the hook'. But grace is so much more. Luke 2:39-41 tells us about what Jesus was like as a child. It says,

> *"When Joseph and Mary had done everything required by the Law of the Lord, they returned to Galilee to their own town of Nazareth. And the child grew and became strong; he was filled with wisdom, and the grace of God was on him." (NIV)*

Jesus was perfect He didn't need to be let off the hook for anything, and if anyone deserved favor, it was Him. However, this text says the grace of God was on Him. Clearly there's a deeper meaning of grace.

John 1:14-16 gives us even more insight into this amazing concept. It says,

> *The Word became flesh and made his dwelling among us. We have seen his glory, the glory of the one and only Son, who came from the Father, full of grace and*

truth. (John testified concerning him. He cried out,
saying, "This is the one I spoke about when I said, 'He
who comes after me has surpassed me because he
was before me.'") Out of his fullness we have all
received grace in place of grace already given. (NIV)

Jesus was full of grace and because He was full of it, we all get a new grace to replace the grace we already had—What? This passage seems a little confusing. How was Jesus full of grace? Why do we need new grace, was there something wrong with the old grace? As I've thought deeply about this and asked the Holy Spirit for direction, I've come to understand that Jesus' life showed a new facet of grace that was previously unrevealed. This aspect is really *God's supernatural power to do what we're incapable of on our own.* This aspect of grace helps me understand why the Bible says we're to live in grace (Galatians 1:6), grow in grace (2 Peter 3:18), and be stewards (managers) of God's grace (1 Peter 4:10).

Two men in a church, Paul and William, decided they wanted to become godly men, so they started meeting with one another to pray and encourage one another. They set goals for themselves and their behavior, and were accountable each to the other one.

Paul decided he wanted to break his habit of using profanity. He decided he was going to put five dollars in the offering for every time he swore during the week. To stay accountable, he would tell William how many times he'd failed. The first week cost Paul $100. Paul must've been doing okay financially, because that didn't stop his swearing. In fact, while he improved somewhat over the next couple weeks, he really wasn't having the success he wanted and was losing a lot of hard-earned cash.

After the fourth week, William told Paul he had decided the deal needed to be changed for the coming week, but he wouldn't tell Paul how it would change. He said, "Trust me. It will cost you both less, and more." When they met the following Sunday before worship, Paul admitted he'd failed again. William put a hand on his shoulder and said, "Paul, I told you this was going to cost you both less and more. It's called grace."

William took out his checkbook, and made out a check to the church, leaving the amount blank. He gave the check to Paul and said, "Your sin still costs, but for you it's free. Fill in the numbers. And next week there'll be more grace." William's grace cost him $55 the first week; the second only cost him $20. There was no third week. Paul couldn't bear to see what his swearing was costing his friend, so he quit.

Grace doesn't just 'let you off the hook'. The penalty is paid, just not by you. Grace also pushes us to stop sinning and live righteous lives. The illustration falls short here. Grace doesn't just give us the *will* to stop sinning; it gives us the *power* to stop sinning. In fact, it gives us the power to do and to be everything God wants us to be.

Grace is so amazing and multifaceted I could easily write a complete book on the topic. Perhaps I will someday, but for now, I am going to zero in on a particular aspect I think can powerfully change your everyday life.

My definition of this aspect of grace is: *God's miraculous power to transform and empower*. Reread that last sentence and let it soak in. Philippians 4:13 says,

> "*I can do all this through him who gives me strength.*"
> *(NIV)*

This aspect of grace gives you the power to do all things. This includes keeping the law of God perfectly. Please understand me; I am not saying to keep God's laws so you can be saved, that's legalism. I am saying Jesus saved you from sin, not just from the effects of sin. His grace is powerful enough to wipe away your past, give you a future in heaven **and** empower you to keep His law in the present. This isn't something you do by your strength, it is His grace which does this through you.

This is good news, because it's living in alignment with God's laws that allows you to thrive in this life. In 1 Corinthians 15:10 the apostle Paul said,

> "*But by the grace of God I am what I am, and his grace to me was not without effect. No, I worked harder than all of them—yet not I, but the grace of God that was with me.*" (NIV)

Paul says that not only did grace make him who he was, but grace did the work he was called to. The apostle Paul did things which are still very much shaping and forming our world today, because he wrote most of the New Testament and was instrumental in bringing the gospel the non-Jewish world. He accomplished more than most people would ever dream of being able to do, and he credits it all to God's grace.

Romans 12:6 is another text illustrating the aspect of grace I am describing. It says,

"We have different gifts, according to the grace given to each of us. If your gift is prophesying, then prophesy in accordance with your faith." (NIV)

According to this verse your spiritual gift is an aspect of God's grace. It's His miraculous power that empowers us to do what we're unable to on our own. Another example of this aspect of grace is found in Acts 4:33-35, which says,

"With great power the apostles continued to testify to the resurrection of the Lord Jesus. And God's grace was so powerfully at work in them all that there were no needy persons among them. For from time to time those who owned land or houses sold them, brought the money from the sales and put it at the apostles' feet, and it was distributed to anyone who had need." (NIV)

In this passage we see God's grace inspired people to do what they would never ordinarily do. Every communist society has tried and failed to accomplish the lifestyle God's grace caused to come easily and naturally.

God's grace takes things that were hard for you, and that you struggled to do — in fact, things impossible for you—and makes them easy. In Matthew 5:48 Jesus said,

> "*Be perfect, therefore, as your heavenly Father is perfect." (NIV)*

This is not possible for us, but it's easy for grace. Grace can do what was impossible.

Do you ever struggle to love someone who sucks the joy out of your life? Someone who's a leach and takes everything you have? Or an enemy you know you should love, but who continually harasses and annoys you? Ask God for the grace to love them. Or maybe you struggle with some sin in your life. You want to be free of it, but you keep falling back into it, and no matter how hard you try, you can't seem to get free. You need to ask God to let

His grace rule that area of your life. Because we're not under the law, but under grace.

What do we do if we ask God to change some aspect of our lives and nothing seems to happen? It seems we aren't any better than we were before. We asked God to give us the power to be an exceptional preacher and share His word, but we still get stage fright and can hardly say a word when we get in front of people. What then?

2 Corinthians 12:9 says,

"My grace is sufficient for you, for my power is made perfect in weakness." (NIV)

Grace takes our weaknesses and transforms them. It isn't your job to change your weaknesses and failures. It's your job to submit to God and let Him work His grace through your life. When it seems like a slow process and you aren't making much progress, remember God is the one who's responsible for your transformation and He will finish the work He started in you. In the meantime, learn to rejoice in your weaknesses and failings, knowing that in doing so you're bringing glory to God.

There's an old fable from India I heard recently. A water bearer had two large water pots, which he carried on either end of a pole slung across his shoulders. One pot had a crack in it, so every day as he carried water to his master's house he arrived with one full pot and one only half full. This went on for two years. One pot was very proud of its accomplishments, while the imperfect pot was embarrassed at its failure. Its distress at being able only to accomplish half of what it had been made to do resulted in its speaking one day to the water carrier.

"*I am so ashamed,*" the pot said. "*Why?*" asked the carrier. "*Because water leaks out all the way to your master's house and because of my crack I've been only able to deliver half of the load.*" The water carrier looked kindly at the cracked pot and said, "*As we return to my master's house today, I want you to look at the beautiful flowers along the path.*"

The beauty he saw along the way cheered the pot. "*Did you notice the flowers were only on your side of the path?*" the water carrier asked. "*I've always known about your flaw, and I took advantage of it. I planted seeds on your side of the track and as we walked back each day from the stream, you watered them. For two years I have been able to pick fresh, beautiful flowers for my master's table. Without your being exactly the way you are, this beauty wouldn't have graced his house.*"

God has made His grace freely available to each of us. It's like money in the bank. All we've to do is access it. The spiritual debit card that lets us draw on this incredible resource is faith. Faith isn't something we have to manufacture either. God gives us faith — we simply have to choose to exercise it. When we exercise our faith, it grows. Asking God for His grace is the first step of faith. The second step is to believe we have it and to act accordingly. Finally, look for the '*flowers*' that are growing around us as God's grace empowers us and transforms our weaknesses into rich blessings.

Chapter Two

Banish the Bad Emojis

Growing up, my mother was in constant fear of every disease and illness known to humanity. It didn't help that she was a nurse and daily saw all the terrible things that could go wrong. Every time she opened a can, she made us be quiet so she could hear if it made a *pshh* sound. If it didn't, she would throw it out in fear of getting botulism. If a squirrel got to close to us at the park, she would freak out that we could get rabies or bubonic plague from it. But her biggest fear was cancer. We were one of the last families to get a microwave because she was convinced it would cause cancer.

When I was in Jr. High, her worst fear came true when a doctor diagnosed her with cancer. Then a miracle happened. God didn't heal her of cancer, but He healed her spirit of worry and anxiety. I watched my mother go from being worrier to be warrior. She was joyful and at peace during the entire course of the illness that eventually took her life. She traveled around sharing her testimony and giving praise to God in the middle of her trial.

I miss my mother terribly, but I am determined to carry on her legacy by proclaiming her truth: "***It is possible to leave behind fear, anxiety, stress and many types of anger and instead live in perfect joy and peace***." I know this sounds like pie-in-the-sky, but it should be the norm. I am confident in proclaiming—anyone can be free of anger and anxiety and can receive joy and peace. Not because I think so, not even because of my experience or because of a scientific study. No, I am confident you can learn to leave behind fear and anxiety and receive joy and peace because God says you can. The Bible repeatedly commands us not to fear and not to be anxious. In fact, it says it 365 times - one for each day of the year. Here's a small sampling.

Philippians 4:6 says,

> *"Do not be anxious about anything, but in every situation, by prayer and petition, with thanksgiving, present your requests to God." (NIV)*

In John 14:27 Jesus is leaving his disciples with some last instructions before He goes to the cross and then is resurrected and ascends to heaven. Immediately after He shares the last supper with His disciples, He tells them,

> *"Peace I leave with you; my peace I give you. I do not give to you as the world gives. Do not let your hearts be troubled and do not be afraid." (NIV)*

Jesus wouldn't have told us not to let our hearts be troubled or be afraid if He wasn't also providing a way for us to get to that place. So how can we make that a reality in our lives? The secret to is allowing Jesus to be not only Savior but Lord.

Jesus came and died on a cross so we could enjoy eternal life with Him in heaven. That isn't all, He also came so we could enjoy an abundant life now. Both things only happen when we allow Him to be in total control of our lives. We must turn over the reins to Him and let Him be the boss. That may not sound very fun; we enjoy being in control of our own decisions. But I have found it to be the best decision anyone can make. In John 10:10 Jesus says,

> "*The thief comes only to steal and kill and destroy; I have come that they may have life, and have it to the full.*" (NIV)

When Jesus talks about having life to the full, He isn't just referring to our future in heaven. He wants us to have that abundant life now. By putting Him in charge of our life, we can thrive now.

Please don't misunderstand me, that doesn't mean that Jesus is going to shower us with money. Jesus said blessed are the poor, so His blessing of our lives doesn't necessarily mean money. In fact, money can be a curse for many people. Jesus wants you to have a life of true abundance; a life rich with relationships, positive emotions, physical and mental health, and most of all spiritual vitality. Later in this book I will reveal the principles for achieving financial wealth that will work for anyone, but for those who really understand life, finances are the least important thing. I want to teach how to gain wealth in the things that really matter. Think about it this way. Would you rather be poor and happy, or rich and miserable? Most people think money would make them happy, but the insanely high suicide rate among lottery winners shows otherwise. So instead of beginning by talking about how you can get money, let's talk about your emotional life. How can you banish or heal negative emotions and release joy and peace in your life?

Before we get into that, allow me to ask a question. What is the purpose of emotions? Have you ever wondered why we have them? I mean, it seems like emotions get us into a lot of trouble. Perhaps the world would be a better place if we were all like Spock on star trek and made all our decisions completely rationally. Why did God create us with emotions?

I believe that there are two reasons. First, God meant for them to help guide us and connect us with Him. Some may think I've lost my mind when I say that. I can hear the voices exclaiming, *"What? No! never trust your emotions! Use logic, reason, and the Bible to guide you."* No doubt someone is already thinking of Jeremiah 17:9 which says, *"The heart is deceitful above all things."* This text was talking about our old heart, but God promises in Ezekiel 36:26 to give us a new heart.

"I will give you a new heart and put a new spirit in you; I will remove from you your heart of stone and give you a heart of flesh." (NIV)

God wouldn't give us a deceitful heart. Once we've accepted the new heart God offers we must learn to be ruled by our heart and not our head. The problem with the old heart was that it was hard, it wasn't open to the promptings of the Holy Spirit. When we submit to His Lordship, God gives us a new heart that responds to His promptings. He gives us new spiritual emotions and we need to learn to let them guide us alongside the Bible and logic. These things should work together and complement each other.

Our society idolizes the mind and the self-directed person. It teaches us to set our own destiny; to use logic and reason to set our course and be successful. But God wants our life to be submitted to Him and to His rulership. Jesus lives in our hearts, so His primary connection to us is through our emotions, not through our head.

I am talking about our new heart, not our old heart. This new heart is something you can trust to lead your decisions. If we let our old heart control our lives, our lives are going to be a mess. Proverbs 3:5-6 says to, "*Trust in the Lord with all your HEART* (emphasis supplied — we don't trust God with our mind) *and lean not on your own understanding.*" Don't rely on logic, reason, or your own ideas of what will work. "*In all your ways acknowledge Him and He will direct your path.*" *(NIV)* If we trust God with our heart, He will help us know which way to go. But how will He lead us? He will lead us with our heart - our new heart!

If you live from your new heart, your life is going to line up with what God wants, but your brain is going to be in rebellion against this. It will scream, "This is crazy, listen to me." As the Bible says,

> "*The person without the Spirit does not accept the things that come from the Spirit of God but considers*

them foolishness, and cannot understand them

because they are discerned only through the Spirit."

1 Corinthians 2:14 *(NIV)*

On the flip side, look at how God views all our smart ideas, our scheming, so our lives will work out the way we plan.

*"For the wisdom of this world is **foolishness** in God's sight. As it is written: 'He catches the wise in their craftiness.'" 1 Corinthians 3:19 (NIV—emphasis supplied)*

Most Christians have difficulty hearing God's voice. If I were to take a poll, I would guess half of the people reading this would say that they seldom or never hear God's voice. Even among those who do hear God's voice, I don't know very many people (myself included) who would say that they hear Him speaking all the time every minute of every day.

Which is the goal, but I for one can't say that I am there yet. But if Jesus is truly going to be Lord of my life than He has to be Lord of the little things, not just the big things — like if I am going to have dessert based on what He wants. There are some Biblical principles I can apply in making those decisions, but I'm still deciding not Jesus. I'm taking into account all the things I have learned from scripture, but in the end I'm still using my logic and reason to decide what I should do.

What else can I do, though, if I don't hear God telling me to eat the cheesecake or don't eat the cheesecake? I can let my new heart tell me.   So how does my heart speak to me? Through my emotions. Some of you are thinking: "*If I listen to my emotions to find out if I should eat chocolate I am going to be 600 pounds, because my emotions are always telling me to eat chocolate!*" Those are the emotions of your old heart, however, or what the Bible calls the flesh. God has given us a new heart, and since He is spirit, our new heart is a spiritual heart with spiritual emotions. In Romans 8:6 God tells us,

> *"The mind governed by the flesh is death, but the mind governed by the Spirit is life and peace." (NIV)*

When our fleshly emotion influences our thinking, it leads to death. But if the Spirit controls our thinking, we have life and peace. So how do we know if our mind is under the control of the Spirit? We have life and peace. What is peace? It is a Spiritual emotion only found in God. That is why

> *"There is no peace... for the wicked." Isaiah 48:22 (NIV)*

I doubt you think of yourself as a wicked person, but from God's standpoint, we are all wicked without His power to transform us. None of us can find peace apart from God. We have peace only because of what Jesus has done. Romans 5:1 makes it clear that He is the reason for our peace. It says,

*"Therefore, since we have been justified through faith, we have **peace** with God through our Lord Jesus Christ" (NIV emphasis supplied)*

Isaiah 53:5 tells us Jesus made peace possible by His death,

*"But he was pierced for our transgressions, he was crushed for our iniquities; the punishment that brought us **peace** was on him, and by his wounds we are healed." (NIV emphasis supplied)*

From the time we give our life over to Jesus and accept Him as Lord and Savior, His peace descends on our life. It is a gift from God to allow us to thrive amid a chaotic world. Jesus says to us,

"Peace I leave with you; my peace I give you. I do not give to you as the world gives. Do not let your hearts be troubled and do not be afraid." John 14:27 (NIV)

Peace is an emotion that doesn't exist in your natural heart, it only comes from the Holy Spirit; therefore, it is an emotion that you can trust to guide your decisions both big and small. In fact, the Bible explicitly tells us to be ruled by peace.

> "Let the **peace** of Christ rule in your hearts, since as members of one body you were called to **peace**. And be thankful" Colossians 3:15 (NIV—emphasis supplied)

How do we let peace rule our life? Peace can keep us from doing some things or push us to do other things. It can also help us learn to recognize God's voice. Let's break this down. The opposite of peace is fear. There are many people who probably wouldn't admit it, but they're led by fear. We've probably all experienced that at some point in our lives. This a kind of bondage that the enemy is always trying to get people to fall into. But those experiences can act as teachers for us, since being led by peace happens basically the same way, only with a spiritual instead of a fleshly emotion.

If we stopped and thought about it, we could probably all think of examples where we decided to do or not do different things based on fear. I know people who married someone they knew wasn't right for them because they were afraid that they were going to end up old and alone. Other people chose the career they did not because they enjoy it or have any passion for it, but because they were afraid of not making enough money to take care of their family if they did what they were passionate about. I've met people who refuse to fly on an airplane, making it so they rarely get to see some of their family members because they live far away and they won't fly.

Fear is also a teacher to let you know how to recognize the voice of the liar. Some people believe all the thoughts in their head are their own. But that's just not true. We have the words of our enemy, God's words, and our own thoughts all there together. The sooner we can learn to figure out who's who, the better our life will be. A simple place to start in figuring that out is to notice who speaks things to your heart that make you afraid.

Perhaps your loved one is two hours late getting home and not answering their cell phone. You picture them dead at the side of the road, and all the different what ifs begin going through your mind. That's the enemy doing that to you. He will often suggest a course of action to act on the fear He put in your heart. You may have a thought like, "I won't be able to pay my bills, why don't I skip tithing this month? God knows I need to get my car fixed and I don't have money for both. I'm sure he will understand."

Fear doesn't decide, but it works with the mind to lead us into making a certain decision if we let it. Peace works the same way. God wants us to get to a place in our life where we live in total and constant peace. He promises that He,

> "*will keep in perfect peace those whose minds are steadfast, because they trust in you.*" Isaiah 26:3 (NIV)

Having a steadfast mind means that we don't entertain thoughts of fear or other negative emotions and thoughts. We take every thought captive as the Bible commands and think about positive, uplifting things. Philippians 4:8 says it this way,

> "*Finally, brothers and sisters, whatever is true, whatever is noble, whatever is right, whatever is pure, whatever is lovely, whatever is admirable—if anything is excellent or praiseworthy—think about such things.*" (NIV)

God gives us His supernatural peace, but we have to learn to live in it by consciously choosing to turn our thoughts away from fear and anxiety to whatever is good and pleasant. Then the peace of God guards our heart and mind.

When peace is my normal state of being, and suddenly I feel uneasy, it may be a check from God's Spirit reaching me. Then I think, "*Oh, I better not do what I was about to do, because I don't have peace about it.*" Then if I ignore that check and try to reason and use my mind to convince myself and God that what I'm about to do is okay, then I seriously lose my peace. If I still ignore it, I may experience negative consequences and go, "*Oh, that was God trying to warn me not to go down that road. I guess next time I should listen.*" That's one way I train myself to hear what God's voice sounds like.

To summarize: one of the reasons God gave us emotions is to help guide us. I've spent emphasized this because I want to demonstrate that submitting to God and allowing Him to give us a new heart is how we release the positive emotions of love, joy and peace. Galatians 5:22-23 says,

> *"But the fruit of the Spirit is love, joy, peace, forbearance, kindness, goodness, faithfulness, gentleness and self-control. Against such things there is no law".* (NIV)

The positive emotions of love, joy, and peace grow in our lives along with the other fruits of the Spirit as we continually learn to deepen our relationship with God.[1]

So far, we have learned that God gave our emotions to help guide us and that we can release joy and peace in our lives by allowing the Spirit to live and grow in our

---

[1] IF YOU WOULD LIKE TO LEARN MORE ABOUT HOW DEEPEN YOUR RELATIONSHIP WITH GOD, I WOULD ENCOURAGE YOU TO CHECK OUT MY BOOK GOD'S SUBMARINES WHICH IS AVAILABLE ON AMAZON, BARNES AND NOBLE, APPLE BOOKS, AND MANY OTHER PLACES.

hearts. But how do we banish or heal negative emotions, and what is the other reason God gave us emotions?

The second reason God created us with emotions is because He Himself has emotions and He created us in His image. God experiences most of the emotions we experience. There are few emotions that He doesn't experience, and these are actually the ones He commands us not to have. God never experiences fear or anxiety. Think about it, what could ever make God fearful? He already knows the future; He is all powerful, so what could He fear? Why would He be anxious?

I could ask the same question of us. We have a heavenly Father who loves us, and holds our future, and is all powerful — so why would we ever be anxious or fearful? But we are. Which begs the question, if we're created in God's image and He doesn't experience fear, where does fear come from? I believe that fear, like all sin, is simply an absence of something that should be there.

Perhaps I'd better pause and explain what I mean by that. Sometimes people say that if God created everything that means He created evil and is therefore some kind of monster. But the hole in that theory is that evil isn't a thing. In the same way, that darkness isn't a thing. You can't measure darkness; you can't shovel darkness out of the room. Darkness isn't a thing, it is the absence of light. In the same way, evil isn't a thing; it is the absence of good. Evil cannot exist without good. If there was no good, then there would be an absence of everything -which is nothing. Evil is an absence of a good that should be there. For example, a dead rock isn't evil, but a dead child is. A rock shouldn't be alive, a child should. Without there first being a good that should exist, there can't be evil.

In the same vein, fear is the absence of faith. God didn't create fear, fear results from the absence of faith. Sometimes I toss my daughter gently into the air. Don't call DCF, I am careful and she loves it. In fact, she smiles and laughs. Why? She knows I am going to catch her. That is faith. Hebrews 11:6 says,

> *"And without faith it is impossible to please God, because anyone who comes to Him must believe that He exists and that He rewards those who earnestly seek Him." (NIV)*

It pleases God when we have faith. When we learn to live in constant faith, we won't experience fear Yes, God created our bodies to respond with certain hormones when we face dangerous situations. Those hormones heighten our awareness and make us more alert and ready to respond to anything. That is a good thing, but it is not fear. For example, many people get a queasy feeling when they are on a tall ladder or standing at the edge of a cliff. It makes them more aware of their surrounding and careful with where they step. I say many people, because not everyone has that reaction to heights. I know this because I never did. I love rock climbing, but I never did it for the thrill that some people talk about getting from it. I just enjoy the challenge of trying out new moves and trying to puzzle out how to get past a difficult section. I love the physical challenge of it. However, after forgetting to clip in and falling twenty-five feet I truly appreciate how that feeling can help you be more mindful.

Sometimes it is appropriate to feel an adrenalin rush, but that is only when you are facing imminent physical danger. Even then, we should immediately turn to God and exercise our faith. When the Bible says not to fear it isn't talking about never getting a shot of adrenalin. It is referring to anxiety, generalized fear, fear of the future, fear of what others think of us, etc. When we live in a constant state of elevated adrenalin, it causes a lot of physical problems. Fear causes stress, and chronic stress is one of the leading causes of heart disease, cancer and other major illnesses. The good news is that you can live a life free from those kinds of fears.

How should you handle things when you get that instant shot of adrenalin, when something scary happens? Sometimes, the danger is real and you need to take that adrenalin and use it to run away or fight. Even in that moment, however, you need to be praying and asking God to take control. Many times, the danger is not real. In those instances, I recommend you go get some exercise as soon as possible and get that adrenalin out of your system. Other times you may just need to reframe the emotion and change your mindset. What do I mean by that? Well, let me ask you - what is the difference between the feeling of fear and the feeling of excitement? It really comes down to your mindset—the same hormones are flowing through your body; it's just about how your brain interprets those sensations.

I worked at a summer camp for several summers and there were kids who were scared to death of the rope swing, the high dive, riding horses, waterskiing, or some other activity. When they faced their fears and did the activity anyway, it would often become their favorite thing. They would invariably love it more than anyone else and want to do it over and over. Why? Because they still get the same feeling, but now their brain says, "*I did this and nothing bad happened, therefore, the sensation I am experiencing now isn't fear, it's excitement and joy.*" The people good at reframing the emotion of fear as excitement are the ones who enjoy skydiving.

Okay, so reframing is fine for those momentary bursts of adrenalin, but how do we go about banishing stress, anxiety, worry and generalized fear from our life? Philippians 4:6-8 tells us how.

> "*Do not be anxious about anything, but in every situation, by prayer and petition, with thanksgiving, present your requests to God. And the peace of God, which transcends all understanding, will guard your hearts and your minds in Christ Jesus. Finally, brothers and sisters, whatever is true, whatever is*

noble, whatever is right, whatever is pure, whatever is

lovely, whatever is admirable—if anything is excellent

or praiseworthy—think about such things." (NIV)

The text tells us not to be anxious but instead to pray and to give thanks. So, when I feel anxious, I pray and give the problem over to God. Then I praise Him for all the ways He has and is taking care of me. This text reminds me that when I do that peace guards my heart. God's peace is with me so strongly that it wards off all fear and guards my mind too, so I don't get sucked into negative thoughts.

Chapter Three

Living With Your Emotions

A woman once asked me to endorse her relationship with a married man. Her conscious was obviously bothering her, and she was clearly hoping I'd tell her it was okay. She went on about how his marriage was basically over and he didn't love his wife anymore. She was completely in love with this guy and it felt right. He made her happy. Her central arguments were: it was true love—so it must be from God, and he made her happy. God wants her to be happy, doesn't He?

I didn't endorse their relationship, but what about her premise that God wants her to be happy? I hear this argument for many questionable things, and they rarely work out well. Here she didn't listen to me, or herself because she admitted God told her to stay away from this guy. She dated the jerk who, predictably, broke her heart. She ended up blaming God for letting her heart be broken.

One could argue God wanted her to be happy, and that's why He told her to stay away from the guy. There's truth in that statement, but I also believe God's more concerned with our **holiness** than He is with our *happiness*.

What exactly is God's desire for our emotional life? Does He care about our emotions at all? As previously mentioned, God is an emotional God. 1 John 4:8 says,

> *"Whoever does not love does not know God, because God is love" (NIV)*

Love isn't one of His many attributes like His holiness and omnipotence. Love is the very essence of who God is, it's the core of His identity. Love is a multifaceted emotion, but it's an emotion. Yes, it's also a decision we make to put someone else's needs ahead of our own. Yes, it's also an action, but let's consider love as an emotion. As an emotion, what does the fact that God is love tell us about Him? First, it tells us God is an emotional being.

It also gives us insight into what motivates God's actions. His decisions and activities all flow out of Love. Emotions push us to act on the decisions we make. There've been some sad cases where individuals had a brain injury, either through a traumatic event or the removal of a tumor, and they couldn't make decisions. They seemed fine; their IQ was unaffected. They gave rational and reasoned responses why a decision was the most logical, but they couldn't decide. It ended up costing them their jobs and several close relationships. What researchers finally realized was they had lost their ability to experience emotions.

Without the emotions to push them to action, they couldn't act on what they rationally knew was the best decision. What researchers are discovering is that we need emotions to push us into action. So, the fact that God is love also informs us He's a God of action. His love compels Him to act. We see this in Jesus' life. Matthew 14:14 offers us one example.

> "And when Jesus went out, He saw a great multitude; and He was moved with compassion for them, and healed their sick." (NKJV)

There are several more examples, but I think one more will suffice. Mark 1:41 reads,

> *"Then Jesus, moved with compassion, stretched out His hand and touched him, and said to him, 'I am willing; be cleansed'." (NKJV)*

Compassion is love expressed towards those who're hurting and weak. To be moved by compassion means to be propelled towards actions by the emotion of love for someone who's vulnerable and broken. Jesus' love propelled Him into action. We understand intuitively that emotions move us to action. It's expressed in the way we talk about things. If I watch a movie or read a book evoking a strong emotional response, I often say it was very moving.

That's the reason relief organizations show us pictures of starving and hurting children around the world. They want to move us with compassion and help us decide to donate to their organization. They could simply tell me there are 1 million people in Syria who're in danger of starving or freezing to death if I don't help. However, I'm much less likely to have my emotions engaged if I only hear those facts verses seeing the children who're dying. They aren't manipulating my emotions for no reason; most people won't do anything to help unless their emotions are engaged.

God designed us with emotions which will spur us into action. The problems happen when we let our emotions tell us *what* action to take. We need our reason and our emotions to work together. Our emotions should be a gauge which tells us when something's wrong or needs to change. Our *reason* should tell us what to do while our *emotions* push us into carrying it out.

So how does this work? Well, first we have to pay attention to our emotions. We need to recognize we're experiencing an emotion and identify it. Sometimes it's easy for us to so focus on a task or direction that we ignore the way we're feeling. Our emotions are desperately trying to tell us something, but we can be deaf to them. When this happens, not only do we miss out on the opportunity to gain insight into whatever situation we're facing, but those emotions continue to build up and cause our bodies to be in a continual state of upheaval. We need to practice being continually aware of our emotions. We must stop and ask ourselves, "What am I feeling?" and, "Why am I experiencing this emotion?"

I am convinced all of our emotions spring from either love or fear. If an emotion is being driven by love, God may use it to prod us into action. If the emotion is being by fear, we may need to change our thought patterns to bring them into line with God's truth.

In the previous chapter I wrote that God experiences every emotion we do except fear. 1 John 4:18 tells us,

> *"There is no fear in love. But perfect love drives out fear, because fear has to do with punishment. The one who fears is not made perfect in love." (NIV)*

If your emotions are rooted in fear, go back and reread what I wrote in the previous chapter on dealing with fear.

Let's look at two opposite emotions: sadness and happiness, and their cousins grief, depression, elation, and joy. What exactly is sadness, and how's it derived from love or fear? Sadness at its core is a deep yearning for something missing in our life. It could be something we once had and lost, which causes grief. It could be something we're created to enjoy but never have experienced. But can sadness come from love? God is love, so another way to ask this question is to ask: does God ever experience sadness?

Matthew 26:36-37 says,

> *"Then Jesus went with his disciples to a place called Gethsemane, and he said to them, 'Sit here while I go over there and pray.' He took Peter and the two sons of Zebedee along with him, and he began to be sorrowful and troubled. Then he said to them, 'My soul is overwhelmed with sorrow to the point of death. Stay here and keep watch with me.'" (NIV)*

The Bible describes Jesus as overwhelmed with sorrow to the point of death... this sounds like deep depression. So Jesus certainly experienced sadness. Isaiah 53:4 tells us He carried all our sadness. It says,

> *"Surely he has borne our griefs and carried our sorrows; yet we esteemed him stricken, smitten by God, and afflicted." (ESV)*

pg. 74

According to Ephesians 4:30 the Holy Spirit can be grieved (made overly sad) by our actions.

"And do not grieve the Holy Spirit of God, with whom you were sealed for the day of redemption." (NIV)

God experiences sadness, so it must be possible to flow from love. But how? To answer this question, we need to understand that the opposite of love isn't hate; the opposite of love is apathy — the absence of all emotion. If we had no emotion for something, there'd be no sadness at its absence. The sadness we feel shows the love we have for a relationship that was lost or the yearning we have to be loved in a particular way. I say lost relationship, but it actually could be a lost or missing aspect of a relationship that's making us sad. For instance, if you and your spouse have drifted apart and no longer share the same level of intimacy you once did, there can be sadness which develops over that loss even though the relationship continues and may even be healthy in other areas.

This is an excellent illustration of what I was talking about earlier when I said we need to pay attention to our emotions and allow them to push us into action. If you developed this sadness and didn't stop to notice you were feeling sad, and ask yourself why, the emotion would continue to build and fester. Eventually, it could cause you to develop bitterness and anger towards your spouse without ever knowing why.

On the other hand, if you attended to the emotion and realized, "*Hmmm, I'm feeling sad, let me check in with my heart and see what's going on. Oh, it's a longing for a deeper level of conversation and intimacy with my spouse; let me plan for how I can make this a reality in our marriage,*" then you'd be prodded into action.

Nobody enjoys feeling sad. We try to avoid it at all costs. We distract ourselves with activity to avoid having to face this emotion. However, this is a self-defeating tactic. Matthew 5:4 says,

Happy are those who mourn;

God will comfort them! (GNT)

Many translations render the word happy as blessed because this seems like an oxymoron, but the Greek word definitely included the idea of being happy. Jesus is saying if you want to be happy don't ignore your sadness; allow yourself to mourn for what you have lost and let God comfort you.

One way I allow God to comfort me is to travel back to the time of loss in my imagination, and I ask God to show me what He was doing in my life during this time. In my mind's eye, I enter that scene and look for Him. I invite God into this process, and He shows me what He was doing. When I see and understand how God was and is working to bring good out of loss, it helps to change my focus and heals my heart. Sometimes this might mean that in my imagination Jesus has His arm around me and He says, "It's okay to cry, I am here with you."

Some may wonder, how long should I mourn? The answer is until you're done. How do you know when you're done? Well, how do you know when you're done going to the bathroom? It's all out. Right? It's the same thing with grieving and sadness. You mourn and grieve until it's all out. There's no set time, it's different for everybody, but you know when you're done.

While you're in this process, you can cling to texts like: Psalm 34:18-19

> *"The Lord is close to the brokenhearted and saves those who are crushed in spirit. The righteous person may have many troubles, but the Lord delivers him from them all" (NIV)*

1 Peter 5:10

> *"And the God of all grace, who called you to his eternal glory in Christ, after you have suffered a little*

while, will himself restore you and make you strong,

firm and steadfast." (NIV)

Psalm 30:5b

"... weeping may stay for the night,
but rejoicing comes in the morning." (NIV)

Sadness can also result from fear instead of love. If this is the case, it requires a unique response. If you've anxiety and fear about the future, it can cause you to develop sadness and even depression. In your mind you've already experienced a future loss, and your emotions are responding to a loss that hasn't even happened yet. There's no amount of grieving that will be enough in this scenario because you're continually experience hypothetical losses.

The answer is to change our thinking and allow God's love to cast the fear out of our life. We can't allow our mind to dwell on worries, stresses, and all the bad things which might happen. How do we do this, however?

Trying not to think about it won't work. We need to redirect our thoughts into proper channels.

2 Corinthians 10:5 says,

> *"We demolish arguments and every pretension that sets itself up against the knowledge of God, and we take captive every thought to make it obedient to Christ." (NIV)*

Taking thoughts captive means we recognize when our thoughts are out of line with God's thoughts, and we learn to replace our thoughts with God's thoughts. We have already established God never experiences fear, so any anxious thoughts aren't from Him. When you recognize you're thinking something that's out of line with God's Word say to yourself, "*That's a lie,*" and then say "*God's truth is:_____*". Now if you aren't sure what God's truth is, ask Him to show you and search the scriptures. Often the lies which keep us captive are the same lies over and over again. So, when you find scriptures which counter the lie with the truth, take the time to memorize them so you can immediately quote them when you need to take a thought captive.

There are many causes for depression, and chronic anxiety is one of them. If you suffer from depression, try using the principles I am talking about, but also seek the services of a good Christian psychologist. It's not a lack of faith to go to a mental health professional to help with your emotional healing any more than it's a lack of faith to go to a medical doctor for physical healing. God can, and does, heal supernaturally, but He also has given professional individuals the knowledge to to help using the scientific principles He set up.

Okay, let's move on to happiness. What exactly is happiness? Webster's Dictionary gives two definitions. One is "a state of contentment", the other is "a pleasurable or satisfying experience". There's this tension with happiness being dependent both on our external circumstances (a pleasurable or satisfying experience) and our internal state (a state of contentment). It's that moment I wish could last forever when everything seems good. It's like being on vacation with no stress or worries and gazing at a beautiful landscape while holding a loved one close. When the moment happens, I'm content and peaceful and I don't want to move and spoil it. I want to stay frozen there in time. Inevitably though, I start to get cold, hungry or have to go to the bathroom. This is the problem with happiness. We only stay content with our circumstances for so long and discontent sets in and we're pursuing the next thing we need to feel content and happy.

Most of us are familiar with the line from the United States Declaration of Independence which says, "*We hold these truths to be self-evident, that all men are created equal, that they are endowed by their Creator with certain unalienable Rights, that among these are Life, Liberty and the pursuit of Happiness.*"

God certainly provides us with life and liberty, and He gives us the freedom to pursue happiness, but does He *want* us to pursue happiness? I contend He wants us to pursue it, but not the way the world does. The world pursues happiness by pursuing the *circumstances* they imagine will make them happy. This won't lead to happiness, because when we realize those circumstances the contentment is only momentary. Then we look for some new circumstance to bring us fulfillment. This means we're always looking forward to some future time when we'll be happy, but failing to enjoy the moment we've right now.

Too many people live their lives like Adam Sandler in the movie "Click". The premise of the movie was that an angel in the "Beyond" part of Bed, Bath and Beyond gave him a remote control that controls actual life. He had the power to pause the entire world or hit fast forward whenever he liked. Every time he didn't enjoy something, he hit fast forward. He fast forwarded most of his life and ended up quickly at the end, realizing that he had skipped his entire life. In fast forwarding the unpleasant parts, he had missed out on real living. We don't have such a remote. But many people check out on everyday life; they aren't engaged in the moment but bury themselves in their smart phones, their work, or their obsession with the future happiness they're working toward. They miss their lives as surely as Adam Sandler's character did in "Click".

This is a sad effect of pursuing happiness in a worldly way. What's the alternative? How would God have us pursue happiness? I propose that there are two ways. There's a supernatural emotion called joy that's one of the fruits of the Spirit. Meaning, joy will flow more and more as the Holy Spirit operates in our lives. Joy is completely independent of our circumstances. It seems paradoxical, but it's possible to have God's joy even amid sorrow and grief. Joy isn't exactly the same thing as happiness, but it's related. It pleases God when we pursue joy by pursuing a deeper relationship with Him.

The second way we can pursue happiness is by pursuing contentment. Remember, Webster's defined happiness both as being in a state of contentment and as having pleasurable experiences. The world focuses on the experiences in pursuing happiness. But God would have us pursue happiness by learning to be content, whatever our circumstances. In Philippians 4:11-13 the apostle Paul says,

> *"I am not saying this because I am in need, for I have learned to be content whatever the circumstances. I know what it is to be in need, and I know what it is to have plenty. I have learned the secret of being content in any and every situation, whether well fed or hungry, whether living in plenty or in want." (NIV)*

Paul discovered the secret to being continuously happy. He's content in all circumstances. Contentment is literally the dictionary definition for happiness. It's the sensation that all is well. Paul says he's figure out the secret, but in this passage he doesn't tell us what it is. However, his advice two chapters earlier is actually the secret. Philippians 2:3-4 tells us not to think about ourselves but to contemplate others, it says,

> *"Do nothing out of selfish ambition or vain conceit. Rather, in humility value others above yourselves, not looking to your own interests but each of you to the interests of the others. (NIV)*

Mark 9:35 describes Jesus giving His secret to greatness,

> *"Sitting down, Jesus called the Twelve and said, 'Anyone who wants to be first must be the very last, and the servant of all.'"*

This is God's secret to greatness. Is greatness the same as happiness? Christine Carter, a PH.D. in psychology, had this to say in the magazine *Psychology Today*

"Compelling research indicates that the pursuit of happiness—when our definition of happiness is synonymous with pleasure and easy gratification— won't ultimately bring us deeper feelings of fulfillment; it won't allow us to live in our sweet spot. Although we claim that the "pursuit of happiness" is our inalienable right and the primary driver of the human race, we humans do better pursuing fulfillment and meaning—creating lives that generate the feeling that we matter.

And how do we do that? How, exactly do we pursue meaning rather than happiness? We establish our connection to something larger than ourselves; we give ourselves to others.

Fortunately, happiness tends to follow meaning. Meaningful activities generate positive emotions and deepen social connections, both of which increase our satisfaction with life. Indeed, much research shows an undeniable connection between happiness and generosity; the happiest people also tend to be the most altruistic." [i]

The research says if we want to be happy, we must focus on making a difference, having a purpose, and helping others. Jesus and Paul both tell us to put others ahead of ourselves. So this is the big secret. If we desire happiness, we must forget ourselves and work to make other people happy. If we try to make ourself happy we may end up being miserable, but if we serve others and try to make their lives better, we'll enjoy great happiness.

Chapter Four

Why Are You Angry?

I enjoy playing board games and am part of a board gaming club that meets regularly in my city. The kinds of board games I enjoy playing are not the ones you're probably thinking of. I like highly strategic games with a lot of moving parts. Recently, something happened at the game club that left me shaking my head.

On this particular night, we were halfway through the game and it was my turn again. I performed all my actions and passed my turn to the next player. Immediately I realized I had forgotten one action, which would've greatly improved my position in the game. I said, "Man, *I can't believe I forgot to...*" The person who owned the game, we'll call him Rick, said, "*Oh, it's fine. Go ahead and perform that action.*"

Doing the action required me to get something from the supply, which was next to the third player whom we'll call Steve. Rick said to Steve, "*Give Timothy a token from the supply*." Steve said, "*No, his turn his done. Too bad.*" I said, "It*'s fine. I understand. No big deal.*" A minute later Steve was performing multiple actions on his turn when he realized he had made a mistake, and so he took back a couple of his actions. Rick immediately jumped in and said, "*No, if you won't allow Timothy to do his action then you can't undo one of your actions. Give Timothy the token. Give it to him!*" Steve responded with a four-letter word. Rick said it was his game, and he didn't have to put up with being cussed at. He said he didn't want to play anymore, and we were putting the game away.

You've probably guessed this chapter is about anger. It's also about jealousy, bitterness, and turmoil. We can't enjoy the abundant life if we're constantly being roiled by these emotions. Let's start with a quick personal inventory. How are your emotions? Are they exactly the way you want them to be? Do you feel joyful, and at peace, or are you in constant turmoil, anxiety and angry?

If you are alive, and not completely stuffing your emotions so far inside that you're numb, then you'll sometimes experience anger. You may handle anger very well, but this doesn't mean you can't do even better. I believe anger can be a tool to help us become more self-aware and push us into passionate action in the very thing God has called us to do. Ephesians 4:31 says,

> *"Get rid of all bitterness, rage and anger, brawling and slander, along with every form of malice." (NIV)*

This text tells us to get rid of all anger. However, just a few verses before in Ephesians 4:26 Paul says,

> *"In your anger do not sin, Do not let the sun go down while you are still angry," (NIV).*

It would seem it's possible to be angry without sinning, so why does he say to get rid of anger? The key is in verse twenty-six, where Paul says not to let the sun go down while you are angry. You can get angry but don't hold on to it. Get rid of it. This is why it says to get rid of all bitterness. Bitterness is what you get when you hold on to anger and refuse to forgive.

I've been telling people for a long time that God experiences all the emotions we do except for fear, which he repeatedly tells us not to allow in our lives. I realized, however, as I was writing this chapter, that bitterness is a second emotion God doesn't experience. Like fear, bitterness is also an emotion God tells us to avoid. Hebrews 12:15 says,

> *"See to it that no one falls short of the grace of God and that no bitter root grows up to cause trouble and defile many." (NIV)*

Matthew 6: 14-15 says,

> *"For if you forgive other people when they sin against you, your heavenly Father will also forgive you. But if you do not forgive others their sins, your Father will not forgive your sin." (NIV)*

When you refuse to forgive others, your own sins aren't forgiven. Can you imagine the weight of darkness you would add to your soul by this? No wonder holding onto anger causes bitterness. God, of course, is quick to forgive as Jonah points out in what I think is one of the most hysterical scenes in the Bible. This is at the very end of the book of Jonah. I will give a quick recap of the story for those who are unfamiliar.

God tells Jonah, who is a prophet in Israel, to go to the city of Nineveh and tell the citizens to repent. Jonah doesn't want to go, so he tries to run away from God.

He takes a ship headed in the opposite direction. A big storm comes up and everyone fears for their lives. They draw lots to see whose fault it is, and Jonah draws the short straw. He confesses he's running away from God and tells them to throw him into the sea. The desperate sailors finally do, and the sea is instantly calm. Meanwhile, Jonah gets swallowed by a giant fish. Jonah spends three days in the fish's belly, which finally vomits him up onto land. He makes his way into Nineveh and tells them to repent or the city will be destroyed. They repent and this leads us to Jonah, chapter four. I am going to quote from The Message Bible because I think it captures the full richness of Jonah's emotions really well.

> "*Jonah was furious. He lost his temper. He yelled at God, 'God! I knew it—when I was back home, I knew this was going to happen! That's why I ran off to Tarshish! I knew you were sheer grace and mercy, not easily angered, rich in love, and ready at the drop of a hat to turn your plans of punishment into a program of forgiveness!*

pg. 94

So, God, if you won't kill them, kill me! I'm better off dead!'

God said, 'What do you have to be angry about?'

But Jonah just left. He went out of the city to the east and sat down in a sulk. He put together a makeshift shelter of leafy branches and sat there in the shade to see what would happen to the city.

God arranged for a broad-leafed tree to spring up. It grew over Jonah to cool him off and get him out of his angry sulk. Jonah was pleased and enjoyed the shade. Life was looking up.

But then God sent a worm. By dawn of the next day, the worm had bored into the shade tree and it withered away. The sun came up and God sent a hot, blistering wind from the east. The sun beat down on Jonah's head and he started to faint. He prayed to die: 'I'm better off dead!'

Then God said to Jonah, 'What right do you have to get angry about this shade tree?'

Jonah said, 'Plenty of right. It's made me angry enough to die!'

God said, 'What's this? How is it that you can change your feelings from pleasure to anger overnight about a mere shade tree that you did nothing to get? You neither planted nor watered it. It grew up one night and died the next night. So, why can't I likewise change what I feel about Nineveh from anger to pleasure, this big city of more than 120,000 childlike people who don't yet know right from wrong, to say nothing of all the innocent animals?'" Jonah 4 (MSG)

I love this story because it helps to illustrate the multifaceted reasons we get angry. Anger isn't a primary emotion. It grows out of other emotions, like embarrassment, fear, frustration, or pain; and in many cases masks those emotions. Therefore, paying attention to our anger can help us grow because it can alert us to emotions we've suppressed. These suppressed emotions can hold us back from really enjoying life, and can also cause a multitude of health problems. Think of anger as the release valve for emotions which aren't being dealt with in healthy ways.

If we get angry often and easily, that's a clear sign there's an underlying emotion needing our attention. Even if you seldom get angry, but you know you've a few key things which can get you wound up, it would benefit you to think deeply about what the underlying emotion is and why you feel this way. Okay, so let's have a little fun and see if we can psychoanalyze Jonah in this story. Verse one says he was furious with God. He gets so mad that God isn't destroying Nineveh, he asks God to kill him instead. How angry do you have to be to want to die? I mean, he has some serious anger management issues!

Let's see if we can figure out what the underlying emotion is that's causing this fury.

One possibility is embarrassment. Jonah didn't tell Nineveh to repent or God will destroy your city. He said God **is** going to destroy Nineveh. Jonah 3:4

> "*Jonah began by going a day's journey into the city, proclaiming, 'Forty more days and Nineveh will be overthrown.'*" (NIV)

Jonah didn't say this was a conditional prophecy; he just said it's going to happen. Jonah could've been accused of being a false prophet. This was one of the largest cities in the known world. Apparently, everyone in the city had heard the prophecy of Jonah. If they didn't hear him directly, they heard the king's decree that resulted from his preaching. Word will get back to Israel that his prophesy wasn't fulfilled, and he might become a laughingstock.

Embarrassment was probably one of the underlying emotions of Jonah's anger, but the rest of the verse gives some clear indications there was a lot more going on. Jonah says, "*I knew this would happen because you are just full of grace and mercy.*" You can sense the anger in his tone with God here. He's basically saying he hates God's grace and mercy. What would drive someone to say something so stupid?

It's clear Jonah didn't like the Ninevites. He would've been happy to see them all burn to death. In fact, he sat up on the hill, still hoping God would go ahead and fry them. Why all the hate? Well, Nineveh was the capitol of Assyria, and the Assyrians were Israel's biggest enemy. Not only were they the strongest empire around, but they were the original state sponsor of terrorism. (This was before Babylon came to power.) They used terror as a weapon. They would approach a walled city and demand the city surrender. If the city surrendered, they might spare some inhabitant's lives, but would scatter them to all the corners of their empire. If the city refused to surrender, when they later defeated the city they would torture the inhabitants in brutal ways and put their corpses on public display as a warning to anyone who would dare oppose them. I don't want to get into all the gruesome details; google it sometime if you're interested.

We don't know if Jonah had any family members who the Assyrians tortured, but it's a probability he at least knew some people this had happened to. You can understand why he didn't want to go to Nineveh and help them get right with God. Jonah probably carries a lot of pain, sorrow, bitterness, and hate, and because of that he gets mad at God.

This is a common thing. When we've unresolved pain, grief, and bitterness in our heart we may often lash out in anger at people who've nothing to do with causing any of it. If we find ourself getting angry at people who haven't really done anything to deserve it, we need to spend some time reflecting on the grief or bitterness that may be in our heart. Then we must ask God to come and heal our hurt.

God grows a whole shade tree for Jonah overnight. Jonah gets happy and apparently doesn't want to die anymore. But then the next night a worm kills the tree and Jonah is so mad again that he wants to die. Talk about serious anger issues! I mean, it's just a plant. His response is completely over the top for what he's actually lost. His anger is clearly stemming from grief over losing the tree. It's natural to grieve when you lose something important to you, and anger is one stage of grief. It's natural to grieve when we lose something important, but when our grief is out of proportion to the loss, it's a sign we still haven't properly dealt with something else. So, to continue to psychoanalyze Jonah here, we'd say he probably has experienced some significant loss in his life prior to this that he hasn't healed from yet.

Anger is like a big 'check engine' light. It's telling us something is wrong and we need to deal with it. Now, there are all kinds of techniques people use to control anger. Some count to ten and then go for a walk. Other people just grit their teeth and smile. But if this is all you do, then it's kind of like unscrewing the lightbulb on your check engine light instead of diagnosing the problem and fixing it.

We like to think the problem is external. We say things like, "He makes me so mad!" which isn't true; nobody can make us mad. We choose to become angry or not. That's not to say we don't have triggers. It's just those triggers are an internal problem and we need to learn to deal with them so nothing can trigger us to anger. James 1:19-20 says,

> "*My dear brothers and sisters, take note of this:*
> *Everyone should be quick to listen, slow to speak and*

slow to become angry, because human anger does not produce the righteousness that God desires." (NIV)

James says human anger doesn't produce the righteousness God desires. Why did he feel the need to put the modifier '*human*' in that sentence? Is there another kind of anger? Yes, there is Godly anger. Nahum 1:3 tells us God is slow to anger. It doesn't say He doesn't get angry; it says He's slow to anger.

Which is why James says we should be slow to anger. He doesn't say, "Don't get angry." He says, "Be slow to anger," because human anger doesn't lead to righteousness. Anger that you come to slowly is Godly anger. You can't be slow to anger if you have triggers. A trigger, by definition, goes off fast. If you have things that trigger your anger it's important to recognize what they are and ask God to help you find healing.

What is Godly anger? John 2:13-17 gives us a glimpse. It says,

"When it was almost time for the Jewish Passover, Jesus went up to Jerusalem. In the temple courts he found people selling cattle, sheep and doves, and others sitting at tables exchanging money. So he made a whip out of cords, and drove all from the temple courts, both sheep and cattle; he scattered the coins of the money changers and overturned their tables. To those who sold doves he said, 'Get these out of here! Stop turning my Father's house into a market!' His disciples remembered that it is written: 'Zeal for your house will consume me.'" (NIV)

If anger is the secondary emotion, what is the primary emotion that's driving Jesus in this passage? It's love for His Father. When our anger is motivated by love, we'll be slow to anger, but it'll also propel us into action. Anger based on love is the fuel for the passion to make a difference in our world. When we see children starving, when we see the poor mistreated, when we see the weak taken advantage of, it should make us angry; and that anger should propel us into motion. If we aren't angry about those things we might need to look in our heart and ask ourself if we've a deficiency of love. Not said in a judgmental, 'I-am-such-a-terrible-person' way. But in a 'God-please-give-me-more-of-your-heart-towards-this-person' kind of way. An apathy towards injustice and pain in our world should be a wake-up call to us that our love has gone cold.

Not incidentally, this is one sign of the end of the world Jesus gave in Matthew 25:12 He said,

> *"Because of the increase of wickedness, the love of most will grow cold." (NIV)*

Jesus said most people will have a deficiency of love in our day. We look around at church and think we are just like everyone else, so we must be doing well. But most people, even in the church, have love that has gone cold. If you aren't angry about the injustice in our world, it's an indicator of something missing in your life. In the same way, being triggered to anger when someone throws a cuss word at you, it's a sign that maybe you've some past hurts that haven't been healed.

My prayer for all my readers is that God will heal you from anything that would trigger you to anger, and you would burn with passion for the things which anger the heart of God. It's this second type of anger that will bring about the abundant life you desire. God's anger propels us into the self-sacrificing service which produces genuine joy in our lives.

Chapter Five

Thank God and Live

When making the outline for this book I strongly considered describing six areas we need to thrive in, instead of only five. The sixth area I thought about covering was our mental state. In the end, I decided it's related closely enough to our emotional and physical aspects that I could include thought life under those umbrellas. In this chapter, I am going to cover the one attitude I believe is the lynchpin for our ability to thrive in every area of life.

I want to begin with a cute story I came across in one of those forwarded Facebook messages that goes around. I am sure it's pure fiction, but that doesn't mean it doesn't contain some valuable lessons.

A man was lost in the desert for five days. One hot day—actually, all desert days are hot—he comes to the home of a preacher. Tired and weak, he crawls up to the house and collapses on the doorstep. The preacher takes him in and nurses him back to health. Feeling better, the man asks the preacher for directions to the nearest town. The preacher tells him the directions, and offers to lend him his horse to make it. The preacher says, "However, there's a special thing about this horse. You have to say 'Thank God' to make it go and 'Amen' to make it stop."

Eager to get to town, the man says, "Sure, okay" and gets on the horse. He says, "Thank God" and sho' nuff, the horse starts walking. Later he says louder, "Thank God, thank God," and the horse trots. Feeling really brave, the man says, "Thank God! Thank God! THANK GOD!" and the horse is soon up to a full run!

About then he realizes he's heading for an enormous cliff and yells "Whoa!" But the horse doesn't even slow! It's coming up REAL QUICK and he's doing everything he can to make the horse stop. "Whoa, stop, hold on!" Finally he remembers "AMEN!!!"

The horse stops a mere two inches from the cliff's edge, almost throwing him over its head. The man, panting and heart racing, wipes the sweat from his face and leans back in the saddle. "Oh!" he says, gasping for air, "Thank God."

This story illustrates the only possible way something bad could ever come out of praising God, and it's a pretty far-fetched story. In all other circumstances, giving thanks to God gives us life and complaining can bring us death.

A Biblical example of this, is the story of what happens right after the 12 spies return from spying out the land of Canaan. I'm quoting from *The Message Bible* because I want you to see this with fresh eyes.

The whole community was in an uproar, wailing all night long. All the People of Israel grumbled against Moses and Aaron. The entire community was in on it, "Why didn't we die in Egypt? Or in this wilderness? Why has God brought us to this country to kill us? Our wives and children are about to become plunder. Why don't we just head back to Egypt? And right now!"

Soon they were all saying it to one another: "Let's pick a new leader; let's head back to Egypt." Numbers 14: 1-4 (MSG)

The Israelites had been slaves in Egypt. The Pharaoh forced them to do hard physical labor for no pay. They built the pyramids with their blood, sweat, and tears. Still, they want to return to Egypt. This isn't the only time, either. Repeatedly, in scripture you see the Israelites talking about going back to Egypt. This is craziness. But before we're too hard on them, we must remember their story is our story.

All of us were slaves in metaphorical Egypt. We were born as slaves to sin. If you've accepted Christ, then He has set you free from bondage to sin. God has promised to bring us into His promised land. But most people are still living in the wilderness. The wilderness represents slavery to fear and old thought patterns. In the wilderness we're free from sin but haven't learned to live by faith. I often see people in this condition looking with jealousy at the people in the world or saying how much easier it was when they weren't Christians. They're wanting to return to Egypt, and some do.

Some people think the Promised Land is heaven. But Canaan cannot represent heaven. In heaven there'll be no enemies and no fighting, but in Canaan there are both. In fact, there are giants in the land of Canaan.

Canaan represents the abundant life God wants for you to live **now**. Canaan means thriving in every area of life. Our Promised Land isn't a piece of real estate; it's a new reality. A thriving life in which "*we're more than*

conquerors through [Christ] who loved us" (Rom. 8: 37 NIV).
A life in which "we do not lose heart" (2 Cor. 4: 16 NIV). A
life in which "[Christ's] love has the first and last word in
everything we do" (2 Cor. 5: 14 MSG). A life in which we're
"exceedingly joyful in all our tribulation" (2 Cor. 7: 4 NIV).
A life in which we're "anxious for nothing" (Phil. 4: 6 NIV),
in which we're "praying always" (Eph. 6: 18 NIV), in which
we "do all in the name of the Lord Jesus, giving thanks to
God the Father through Him" (Col. 3: 17 NIV). Canaan is a
life lived in God's rhythms and under His control.

There are giants in the Promised Land though! The
devil is happy to leave you alone (at least for a while) when
you're a slave to sin. If you find yourself in the wilderness
you'll have problems, but the devil's worst attacks come
when you try to take claim to the Promised Land. I've seen
too many people who weren't expecting this and ended up
wishing they could return to Egypt. Like the Israelites,
some of them try to do just that.

Numbers 14:26-38 describes Israel's experience,

God spoke to Moses and Aaron: "How long is this going to go on, all this grumbling against me by this evil-infested community? I've had my fill of complaints from these grumbling Israelites. Tell them, As I live—God's decree—here's what I'm going to do: Your corpses are going to litter the wilderness—every one of you twenty years and older who was counted in the census, this whole generation of grumblers and grousers. Not one of you will enter the land and make your home there, the firmly and solemnly promised land, except for Caleb son of Jephunneh and Joshua son of Nun.

"Your children, the very ones that you said would be taken for plunder, I'll bring in to enjoy the land you rejected while your corpses will be rotting in the wilderness. These children of yours will live as shepherds in the wilderness for forty years, living with the fallout of your whoring unfaithfulness until the

last of your generation lies a corpse in the wilderness. You scouted out the land for forty days; your punishment will be a year for each day, a forty-year sentence to serve for your sins—a long schooling in my displeasure.

"I, God, have spoken. I will most certainly carry out these things against this entire evil-infested community which has banded together against me. In this wilderness they will come to their end. There they will die."

So it happened that the men Moses sent to scout out the land returned to circulate false rumors about the land causing the entire community to grumble against Moses—all these men died. Having spread false rumors of the land, they died in a plague, confronted by God. Only Joshua son of Nun and Caleb son of Jephunneh were left alive of the men who went to scout out the land. (MSG)

I could sum this up by saying that the way into the Promised Land is through praise, but if we complain, we remain. Notice God calls them wicked because they grumbled. God takes grumbling and complaining very seriously. Why? Because our words have substantial power. Think about this... God said the words "let there be light" and because He said it, the universe is expanding to this day. In fact, God's word is so powerful that when He says something it happens without Him having to do anything else.

His word itself carries the power to create and change anything in the universe. God created us in His image, and so our words also have power. We can't speak things into existence the way He does, but we can release blessings and curses or block them by things we say. Jesus says we'll be judged based on the words we speak. Matthew 12:36-37 warns,

> *"But I say to you that for every idle word men may speak, they will give account of it in the day of*

judgment. For by your words you will be justified, and by your words you will be condemned." (NIV)

Philippians 2:14 commands,

"Do everything without complaining or arguing, "(NIV)

This verse would be a lot easier if it said do most things without complaining. But it says everything. Do the dishes without complaining. Pick up after your spouse or kids without complaining. Clean up the mess other people left in the church kitchen without complaining. Help that person who's always leaching onto you for everything without complaining.

We think we'd be thankful if our life was better. But the truth is, our life would be better if we were more thankful. In fact, even if God worked supernatural miracles for us, it wouldn't be long before we were complaining about the miracles if we haven't changed our complaining spirit.

Look at the Israelites, in Numbers 11:5-6 they complain,

> *We remember the fish we ate in Egypt at no cost—*
> *also the cucumbers, melons, leeks, onions and garlic.*
> *But now we have lost our appetite; we never see*
> *anything but this manna! (NIV)*

Can you imagine, they're complaining about this miracle food God provided from heaven every day. They're all like, "*I am just sick of this miracle. Why can't I have the food the world has? I'm tired of this heavenly stuff.*"

How many times have you complained because you had to clean the house God blessed you with, or repair the car you drive, or wash the dishes you ate off? My grandmother used to have a sign hanging over her sink that read,

> *Thank God for dirty dishes,*
> *They have a tale to tell.*
> *While other folks go hungry,*

We're eating very well.

With home and health and happiness

We should not want to fuss.

For by this stack of evidence,

God is very good to us.

People who're truly thankful don't complain, they find a reason to be grateful. Matthew Henry, who wrote a commentary of the Bible, was robbed one time. The thieves took everything he had. That evening he wrote in his diary these words, "*I am thankful that during these years I have never been robbed before. Also, even though they took my money, they did not take my life. Although they took all I had, it was not much. Finally, I am grateful that it was I who was robbed, not I who robbed.*"

I really believe if we want to change our life, we need to begin by changing our words. We may go to church and praise God, we may thank Him before meals, we may even spend some time each morning getting our praise on, but if we then turn around and complain we're a double-minded person. We need to thank God no matter what's going on in our lives. 1 Thessalonians 5:18 commands us to,

> *"Give thanks in all circumstances, for this is God's will for you in Christ Jesus." (NIV)*

A family gathered for breakfast one morning. The father said the blessing and thanked God for the food. As soon as he said amen he started to grumble about the economy, the poor quality of the food, the way it was cooked, and on and on. His little daughter interrupted him, *"Dad, do you think God heard what you said when you prayed and gave thanks?"* The father answered "*Certainly*". She continued, *"And did he hear what you said about the eggs and the coffee?"* *"Of course,"* answered the father, but with a little less certainty.
Then his daughter asked, *"Dad, which did God believe?"*

James 3:10-12 admonishes,

"Out of the same mouth come praise and cursing. My brothers and sisters, this should not be. Can both fresh water and salt water flow from the same spring? My brothers and sisters, can a fig tree bear olives, or a grapevine bear figs? Neither can a salt spring produce fresh water." (NIV)

Every time we speak negativity and complain we're poisoning the well of our life. This is a poison that brings death. Look at the Israelite experience again. Numbers 21:4-9 tells the story,

"They set out from Mount Hor along the Red Sea Road, a detour around the land of Edom. The people became irritable and cross as they traveled. They spoke out against God and Moses: "Why did you drag us out of Egypt to die in this godforsaken country? No decent food; no water—we can't stomach this stuff any longer.

So God sent poisonous snakes among the people; they bit them and many in Israel died. The people came to Moses and said, 'We sinned when we spoke out against God and you. Pray to God; ask him to take these snakes from us.'

Moses prayed for the people.

God said to Moses, 'Make a snake and put it on a flagpole: Whoever is bitten and looks at it will live.'

So Moses made a snake of fiery copper and put it on top of a flagpole. Anyone bitten by a snake who then looked at the copper snake lived." (MSG)

There are always snakes in the wilderness. But none of them bothered them until they grumbled and complained. Why? Because God was protecting them. But our words have power. When we grumble and complain we're destroying the hedge of protection God has around us and allowing the enemy an avenue to attack us. The serpent the devil is always looking for a way to harm us and when we complain we give him an opening. Now thankfully God is merciful, and when we look at Jesus in faith, even after we have been complaining, He provides a way for us to be healed. But there's going to be a lot of pain and suffering in the process. It's so much better to learn to give thanks in all circumstances.

One of the greatest examples of giving thanks in all circumstances was Fanny J. Crosby. She was the author of over 8000 songs, including several many people still sing today. At 6 weeks of age, Fanny had a minor eye infection. Her parents took her to the Doctor. The doctor used the wrong medicine in her eyes and she became totally and permanently blind.

When she was eight years old, she wrote these words,

> *"Oh! what a happy soul I am!*
> *Although I cannot see,*
> *I am resolved that in this world*
> *Contented I will be.*

How many blessings I enjoy
That other people don't!
To weep and sigh because I'm blind
I cannot and I won't."

Years later, Fanny Crosby said she had no hard feelings against the doctor. In fact, she once said, "*If I could meet him now, I would say thank you over and over again for making me blind.*" She felt her blindness was a gift from God to help her write songs of love and praise.

The Bible commands us to give thanks **in** all circumstances, but a few years ago I made the decision I was going to praise God **for** everything. I wanted to go beyond praising God **in** every situation and actually praise Him **for** everything, even if it seemed terrible.

It wasn't long before my new commitment was put to the test. We were renting a very small home, but it had a beautiful yard with a nice swimming pool. We loved the yard until white flies took it over. White flies are a nasty little insect that swarm like gnats but live on the underside of leaves and drop a sticky substance that molds and turns everything black.

Soon the pool was a nasty brown color and couldn't be used. The pool guy said there was nothing he could do until the white fly problem was under control. The patio, the ground, everything turned black with mold, and the flies made it miserable to be outside. I tried everything I could to get rid of them and pled with my landlord to hire an exterminator. She refused, and I couldn't afford to hire one myself. I got quite grouchy and upset with the situation, but I remembered my commitment and began thanking God for the white flies.

This continued for six months until our lease expired. Because of this problem we started looking at other options and we found a house that was twice the size with a yard that was even better and had no white flies. We rented it for several hundred dollars less than we had been paying for the old house. The white flies ended up being a blessing to us, but I don't think I'd have seen that if I hadn't been thanking God for them all along.

In every situation in life, we have two choices. We can speak life into our circumstances by thanking God and praising Him for what He's doing. Or we can speak death into our life by complaining and grumbling about how bad we have it. I don't know about you, but I know I'd rather give thanks and live!

Chapter Six

Be the Friend You Want

My grandparents were married for over fifty years and often bragged that they'd never had an argument. Some might find this claim incredulous, but if they knew my grandparents, they'd understand. My grandfather is one of the most quiet and meek individuals I have ever met; my grandmother was a very opinionated and forceful woman. My grandfather subscribed to the theory that the secret to a successful relationship is two words, yes dear.

When my grandmother passed away, my grandfather was completely lost. He said, "*I don't know what to wear. She told me what I should wear every day. I don't know what to do. She made my to-do list every day.*" His identity had basically become an extension of hers, and when she died he was completely lost. Long before she died however, he had robbed my grandmother and the rest of us of his presence by allowing his will to be supplanted by hers.

Many people believe that agreeing on everything and having common interests are the foundations for great friendships. The truth is, it is our differences that bring the richness and flavor to our relationships. Imagine if we were all exactly the same: we enjoyed the same activities, thought the same way, and believed the same things. There'd be no reason to talk; we'd already know what the other person was going to say, because they think the same way as us.

I had a girlfriend once who started saying derogatory things to me. She insulted me in front of others and said things that were downright mean. I thought she was just having a bad day and ignored it. But this pattern continued for a few weeks until I finally confronted her about it. I asked, "What's going on? Are you mad at me for something? Why are you treating me this way?" She responded that she was upset with me because I wouldn't argue with her. She told me that if I cared about her, I would argue with her. At the time, I thought that was the dumbest thing I'd ever heard... but I've since come to understand what she was saying. I wasn't trusting her enough to speak up when I disagreed with her; I was falling into the pattern of my grandfather. When she upped the ante by directly insulting me, my silence unintentionally showed that I really didn't care what she thought of me. I was essentially saying, "this relationship isn't worth fighting for."

I don't recommend her tactics, but I am thankful for the lesson I learned—being honest with my genuine feelings and opinions even when I disagree with someone I care about, is foundational to any relationship. One of my favorite quotes is, "*The conversation is the relationship.*" All our friendships are built through conversations — sharing who we are and listening deeply to others.

Delightful conversation actually flows from our disagreements and varying points of view. Therefore, one of the most important relationship skills to learn is how to disagree in a way that builds up rather than tears down.

When my wife Amber and I first got engaged, we began planning our wedding. Like most women, Amber had been dreaming and planning for her ideal wedding since she was a girl. It would've been easy for me to say "Y*ou plan the entire thing the way you want. I'll pay for it and just show up.*" I didn't do that, because I knew that deep down that wasn't what my bride really wanted. She wanted a wedding that would truly be *ours*. We discussed and compromised on *every* detail of the wedding, from her wedding dress to the mints we wanted to serve. My wife has told me many times since that she loved our wedding more than the "perfect" one she had planned out, because it was truly ours. It really represented both of us well. Going through the process helped us learn to communicate and work through our differences in productive and loving ways.

There are four ingredients that go into a great friendship. They are: time together, communication, authenticity and mutual service. (The world confuses mutual service with what they call "chemistry"). Three ingredients (Communication, authenticity, and serving) are skills we can learn. These skills can't be used without the fourth ingredient—time spent together. Relationships take time. We can't make up for lack of quantity with quality. Quality time is important, and you need to be intentional about creating those quality moments for deep connection, but you can't get there without also having a quantity of time. By being present in a person's daily life, you show you are trustworthy. You lay the framework on which those quality time moments can sit. In Genesis 2:2-3 the Bible tells us,

> "By the seventh day God had finished the work he had been doing; so on the seventh day he rested from all

his work. Then God blessed the seventh day and made it holy, because on it he rested from all the work of creating that he had done." (NIV)

God wasn't tired. He didn't rest because they exhausted Him. It was the first full day Adam and Eve were alive. He wanted to spend time with them and set a regular pattern for time together. Ponder that. Adam and Eve's first full day on earth was a day of rest. They hadn't even done anything yet! But God defines rest a little differently than we do. God's rest is all about relationship. Our life and our power come from Him, so when we reconnect with Him it gives us supernatural strength — which is His rest. God prioritizes spending time together so much He dedicated an entire day of creation to carving out that time. We should follow His example and make plenty of time in our life to enjoy relationships.

I've spent considerable time in so-called third world countries. I'm amazed by how much happier many of the poor people in those countries are than many of the people I know here who've plenty. Having spent a year each in two different developing countries, I discovered the pace of life is much slower. They spend a lot more time playing sports, games, and sitting around talking than we do here. I've concluded many of the people in these countries are poor in finances but rich in relationships. Many people here are financially rich but relationally poor. Relationships take time, and in our stressed-out hurried world finding time for people requires work.

Of course, when we go to work, church, school or similar places, we often find ourselves in proximity to people that we haven't chosen to be with. Some relationships seem to just happen because we're placed in proximity to others. On the other hand, when we go to a movie with friends, attend a dinner party or go out on a date, we are being intentional about who we are spending our time with. If we want to thrive, it is important that we use our relational skills to elevate both our chosen and unchosen networks.

The first tool we must use to do that is communication. When we think about great communication, we often think of someone who is articulate and funny, but the most important communication skill is listening well. James 1:19 advises,

> "*My dear brothers and sisters, take note of this: Everyone should be quick to listen, slow to speak and slow to become angry.*" (NIV)

Being quick to listen means being able to take our attention away from distractions and our own thoughts to focus on what the other person is saying. Being slow to speak means we aren't busy planning our reply while others are talking. Instead, we process what they're saying, and then we form a response. One of the best ways to do this is to use what's often called reflective listening. Where we simply say, "*What I hear you saying is...*" and we rephrase what they just told us back to them in our own words. When I first used this technique, it felt wooden and fake. Everything is hard before it's easy, but anything worth doing is worth doing poorly until you can do it well. Today, this comes easily and naturally for me.

What is amazing is how often when I reflect back to a person what they're saying they say, "*No that's not really what I'm saying.*" and then they clarify. If I wasn't using this method, I would have never known that what I heard wasn't what they intended. Proverbs 18:13 says,

> "*To answer before listening—that is folly and shame.*"
> *(NIV)*

This doesn't merely mean answering before you have heard the words; it means to answer before you truly understand what the other person is saying.

Reflective listening helps me to be certain I have really listened before I give an answer. This technique also makes the other person feel heard and valued. When I take the time to confirm with someone that I'm hearing them correctly, it communicates that I value them and what they've to say. In fact, if I don't use this tool, my wife will often say to me, "*What do you hear me saying?*"

The next phase of communication is to go beyond just listening to what the other person is sharing by asking open-ended questions. These may be questions about the person's opinions, feelings, or personal history. People love to share about themselves. When we ask sincere questions, we give people the opportunity to share part of themselves. Research shows that when we share in that fashion, it releases positive endorphins in our brain and makes us feel good. Learn to ask good questions and people will want to be around you because of how you make them feel.

In fact, I came across a story in the New York Times a few years ago titled 36 questions that lead to love. [ii] It cited a study by psychologist Arthur Aron that studied how complete strangers could develop true intimacy by going through these questions together. The thesis was that when someone is interested and listens to you well that it awakens feelings of love in you. On the flip side, sharing personally with others is just as important, because if you haven't been vulnerable in sharing with them they may not be comfortable being transparent with you.

A final thought on communication — when you speak, offer lots of praise, encouragement, grace, and positivity. Colossians 4:6 advises us to,

> *"Let your conversation be always full of grace, seasoned with salt, so that you may know how to answer everyone." (NIV)*

And 1 Thessalonians 5:11 says,

> *"Therefore encourage one another and build each other up, just as in fact you are doing." (NIV)*

Everyone loves to be complimented and encouraged. Practice using these skills and you'll find that people want to be around you. Too often, we say things to make ourselves look good and impress people. But other people aren't thinking that much about us—good or bad. If we want people to like us, it is much better to concentrate on how we make them feel.

The second tool for strengthening our relationships is authenticity. This means allowing others to see the real you. It is putting aside your masks and inviting others into your hopes, fears, inadequacies, and deepest desires. Others may enjoy interacting with the persona you've created, but you will never enjoy a deep friendship with them because the person they're experiencing isn't you. Worse, so many people have been living the lie for so long that they don't even know who their real self is.

A prominent example of this from pop culture is seen in the 2004 movie; ***Mean Girls***. (Spoiler alert!) In the movie there is a group of girls who're known as the "plastics" because they're so over the top fake. These girls terrorize the rest of the school with their gossip and snide put downs. "Cady" played by Lindsay Lohan is a 16-year-old girl who has been home-schooled in Africa for the last 12 years. She gets thrown into this crazy, cliquish high school and has to find her way. In the process, she loses her own identity. She purposely fails math, which she is actually a wiz at, in order to get the attention of a guy. That guy is the ex-boyfriend of Regina, who is the queen bee of the "plastics". This pits Cady against Regina. Cady ends up unseating Regina as the queen bee of the plastics by turning her own tactics against her. I don't want to re-hash the entire plot of the movie but, suffice it to say, that it's only when she embraces her true identity that Cady can enjoy genuine friendship and find a meaningful relationship with the boy she's attracted to.

Cady removed her mask; but so many people never do. They live their entire lives never really allowing anyone to know their true selves. Even those who've never worn a mask and always try to live authentically have blind spots about themselves they're completely unaware of. We can't share with others the things we don't know about ourselves. We each have a deep longing for someone to know us completely and to accept us as we are, but how can this happen when we don't even fully know ourselves?

Thankfully, there's one who knows us better than we know ourselves. Psalm 139:1-4 says,

> "*You have searched me, Lord, and you know me. You know when I sit and when I rise; you perceive my thoughts from afar. You discern my going out and my lying down; you are familiar with all my ways. Before a word is on my tongue you, Lord, know it completely."* (NIV)

God is the person we have been longing for. He knows us completely and accepts us as we are. Not only that, but He can teach us about ourselves. I like to sit in God's presence and invite Him to teach me about myself. I don't always like what He shows me, but it's always true. I can then take the things He reveals and share them with others, which deepens those relationships too.

The last tools for strengthening your relationships are service and submission, which the world mistakenly labels as "chemistry." We're all born with the need for belonging, love, affection and acceptance. When we receive that from someone, it releases many positive endorphins and hormones into our system. It can make us feel like we are floating on the clouds or falling into a gigantic pile of fall leaves. The things that make us feel loved and accepted are different for different people. In his excellent book The Five Love Languages Gary Chapman lists the five primary ways that people experience love; They are: acts of service, words of affirmation, quality time, receiving gifts, and physical touch. There are also unlimited variations of these that he refers to as "dialects". When someone speaks our language, and especially if they speak our dialect we instantly feel an attraction to them because they awaken the feelings of love and belonging that we crave. This is why the world refers to it as chemistry, but the truth is all the love languages and dialects can be learned through careful observation and practice. We serve others by studying them and learning how we can best make them feel loved.

If we want to deepen our relationships, we must be ready to both serve and be served. In John 15:13 Jesus said,

> *"Greater love has no one than this: to lay down one's life for one's friends." (NIV)*

Then in John 13:34 He instructs us,

"A new command I give you: Love one another. As I have loved you, so you must love one another." (NIV)

Jesus loved us by giving His life for us. He commands us to love in the same way He does. We're to give our lives for others. We only have one life, so we can't keep dying repeatedly for our friends! But we can lay down our life in ways other than dying. Your time is your life, so using your time to serve *is* giving your life. Your treasures are the resources, things, or money you've traded your time and energy for. Therefore, you can lay down your life by giving away some of your treasure. Your talents are the skills you've spent your time developing, so you can also give your life by offering your talents in service to others. Whenever you freely offer your time, resources and talents to others instead of using them for yourself, you're laying down your life.

Giving your life for others means you put aside your own desires and ambitions and, instead, serve others. Another way of phrasing this—we must submit to others;

we must put their needs and desires ahead of our own. The love Jesus showed is the same thing as submission. When you understand this, it sheds new light on an often misused portion of scripture. Ephesians 5:21-33 instructs us to,

> *"Submit to one another out of reverence for Christ. Wives, submit yourselves to your own husbands as you do to the Lord. For the husband is the head of the wife as Christ is the head of the church, his body, of which he is the Savior. Now as the church submits to Christ, so also wives should submit to their husbands in everything.*
>
> *Husbands, love your wives, just as Christ loved the church and gave himself up for her to make her holy, cleansing her by the washing with water through the word, and to present her to himself as a radiant church, without stain or wrinkle or any other blemish, but holy and blameless. In this same way, husbands*

ought to love their wives as their own bodies. He who loves his wife loves himself. After all, no one ever hated their own body, but they feed and care for their body, just as Christ does the church — for we are members of his body. 'For this reason, a man will leave his father and mother and be united to his wife, and the two will become one flesh.' This is a profound mystery—but I am talking about Christ and the church. However, each one of you also must love his wife as he loves himself, and the wife must respect her husband." (NIV)

This whole passage starts with the phrase *submit to one another*. Everything Paul wrote after that is an example of how we are to do this. Paul starts with something which was culturally uncontroversial at the time—*Wives submit to your husbands*. He follows this up with a fairly lengthy call for husbands to love their wives the way Jesus loved the church. Remember, this is all an illustration of how we're to submit to one another. The way Jesus loved *is* submission, so this makes sense. We could summarize this passage—Wives submit to your husbands and husbands submit to your wives.

What about the whole 'head of the home' thing? I believe this means that men, as the physically stronger gender who could often force their will in a situation, instead have the responsibility to be a leader and submit first when there is an impasse.   Jesus demonstrated this for us at the last supper. You may remember there was no servant to wash everyone's feet. It was customary for the lowest servant to wash everyone's feet. There were a lot of feet needing washing and nobody was making a move. Nobody would submit to the others and be a servant. John 13 describes how Jesus handled the situation.

> *"Jesus knew that the Father had put all things under his power, and that he had come from God and was returning to God." John 13:3 (NIV)*

Notice the reason Jesus submits and serves is He knew who He was. He knew He had authority and power. Submission is not an act of weakness, but of strength. Jesus said that in the kingdom of heaven whoever wants to be the greatest has to be the servant of all. Jesus knew He was the greatest...

> "*So, he got up from the meal, took off his outer clothing, and wrapped a towel around his waist. After that, he poured water into a basin and began to wash his disciples' feet, drying them with the towel that was wrapped around him.*
>
> *He came to Simon Peter, who said to him, 'Lord, are you going to wash my feet?' Jesus replied, 'You do not realize now what I am doing, but later you will understand.' 'No,' said Peter, 'you shall never wash my feet.'*
>
> *Jesus answered, 'Unless I wash you, you have no part with me.'" John 13:4-8 (NIV)*

This is an important point. To enjoy deeper relationships with others, we need to learn to serve them.

It is also important, however, that we learn to allow others to serve us. We deepen our relationship as much when we let others serve us as when we serve them. Sadly, many people are too proud to allow someone else to offer them any kind of meaningful help. Continuing on with the passage in John 13:9-14 it says,

> "'Then, Lord,' Simon Peter replied, 'not just my feet but my hands and my head as well!'
>
> Jesus answered, 'Those who have had a bath need only to wash their feet; their whole body is clean. And you are clean, though not every one of you.' For he knew who was going to betray him, and that was why he said not everyone was clean.
>
> When he had finished washing their feet, he put on his clothes and returned to his place. 'Do you understand

what I have done for you?' he asked them. 'You call me 'Teacher' and 'Lord,' and rightly so, for that is what I am. Now that I, your Lord and Teacher, have washed your feet, you also should wash one another's feet. I have set you an example that you should do as I have done for you.'" (NIV)

Jesus tells us we should wash each other's feet. He wasn't talking about just doing that as a ritual when we have communion, although that's fine. He was saying we need to constantly and continually submit to each other and serve each other.

There's one ultimate principle foundational to all the other things we have talked about. **Our relationship with God sets the tone for every other relationship we enter.** Ecclesiastes 4:12 says,

"Though one may be overpowered, two can defend themselves. A cord of three strands is not quickly broken." *(NIV)*

We are each stronger with someone else than we are alone, but when we've Jesus in the middle of our friendship then we become a cord of three strands difficult to break. Our relationship with God opens our heart to the possibility of intimacy with others.

When I became a Christian and began to develop a deep relationship with God, it created the possibility to enter other relationships in a deeper way than was ever possible before. There were two reasons for this: First, I learned to know myself better. Psalm 139:1-4 says,

> "O Lord, you have examined my heart and know everything about me. You know when I sit down or stand up. You know my thoughts even when I'm far away. You see me when I travel and when I rest at home. You know everything I do. You know what I am going to say even before I say it, Lord." (NIV)

I don't know everything about myself, but God does! I've forgotten a lot of the things I've done in my life. I don't remember every moment, but God does. There are things about my behavior and motivations I am unaware of. This text says God knows everything about me. This means He knows me better than I know myself. The closer I get to Him, the more self-aware I become and the less self-conscious I grow. God continually reveals things about myself I wasn't aware of before. Therefore, I've more to bring into other relationships and reveal. At the same time, I care less and less about what other people think about me, so I feel safer sharing more things about myself. Knowing God makes me a richer person, able to engage with others in a deeper way.

The second reason my relationship with God allows me to enjoy new depths in my other relationships is being vulnerable with others is less risky because I already have an unbreakable relationship with someone who loves me unconditionally. God knows me completely and still loves me. I typically hide the parts of myself which are sinful, broken, wounded, and ugly or don't measure up to my ideal of what I should be. But God sees all those things and loves me still. Romans 5:8 says,

> *"But God demonstrates his own love for us in this: While we were still sinners, Christ died for us." (NIV)*

God loving me with my imperfections gives me courage to believe maybe someone else could too. It also gives me a solid relationship to fall back on if others reject me.

If you want to strengthen and deepen all the relationships in your life, start with your relationship to God. How do you go about doing that? Well, I wrote a complete book on the subject called <u>God's Submarines</u>. [2] Obviously, I don't have space to cover the whole topic here, but let me give you the highlights. You need a regular and consistent time to meet with God. What

---

[2] Available at Amazon and other book retailers.

should you do with this time? Pray and study the Bible? Yes, but also meditate, listen for His voice, journal, and use your imagination to enter a Bible story or to sit on a hilltop and talk with Jesus. Throughout your day put up scripture and other reminders to turn your thoughts to God. I try to have an ongoing conversation with Him throughout the day. I also make it a habit to ask His opinion before I do or say anything.

In a perfect world, everyone would follow all relationship guidelines God has given us, but we don't live in a perfect world. The sad truth is people will hurt and betray us. How can we keep that fact from ruining our relationships, since our natural tendency is to wall ourselves off to avoid getting hurt again? The answer is: Forgive quickly and easily. Ephesians 4:26 says,

> *"In your anger do not sin: Do not let the sun go down while you are still angry." (NIV)*

Be the Friend You Want

People are going to do things that hurt you and make you angry, but Paul is saying to let it go so quickly that you never go to bed angry. I don't say this in a trite or casual way. Sometimes people do things to us which are hurtful and difficult to forgive. What ends up happening, though, is the unforgiveness in our heart not only poisons our relationship with that person, it poisons all our relationships. Unforgiveness is an infection in our heart which keeps us from fully trusting and engaging with anyone—including God.

Unforgiveness holds more people captive than anything else. This is why Jesus made such a big deal about forgiveness. Matthew 18:21-35 states,

> *"Then Peter came to Him and said, 'Lord, how often shall my brother sin against me, and I forgive him? Up to seven times?'*

Jesus said to him, 'I do not say to you, up to seven times, but up to seventy times seven. Therefore the kingdom of heaven is like a certain king who wanted to settle accounts with his servants. And when he had begun to settle accounts, one was brought to him who owed him ten thousand talents. [A **single talent was worth about $60,000 in today's money—you do the math!]** *But as he was not able to pay, his master commanded that he be sold, with his wife and children and all that he had, and that payment be made. The servant therefore fell down before him, saying, 'Master, have patience with me, and I will pay you all.' Then the master of that servant was moved with compassion, released him, and forgave him the debt.*

But that servant went out and found one of his fellow servants who owed him a hundred denarii;
[Equivalent to a**bout $20,000 in today's dollars, so a significant debt, but not when compared to**

what He'd been forgiven.] *and he laid hands on him and took him by the throat, saying, 'Pay me what you owe!' So his fellow servant fell down at his feet and begged him, saying, 'Have patience with me, and I will pay you all.' And he would not, but went and threw him into prison till he should pay the debt. So when his fellow servants saw what had been done, they were very grieved, and came and told their master all that had been done. Then his master, after he had called him, said to him, 'You wicked servant! I forgave you all that debt because you begged me. Should you not also have had compassion on your fellow servant, just as I had pity on you?' And his master was angry, and delivered him to the torturers until he should pay all that was due to him.*

"So My heavenly Father also will do to you if each of you, from his heart, does not forgive his brother his trespasses." NKJV (brackets supplied)

The king in this story (who represents God) doesn't do the torturing Himself; he turns the man over to the jailor. What this text is saying is that when we refuse to forgive someone we are in a prison of our own making and we will be in torment. It's not like God wants this for us, it is just what will be. In fact, we are our own jailor. We hold the key to freedom: it is forgiveness.

But when someone has abused us, taken advantage of us, stolen something valuable to us, been unfaithful to us, broken our heart, or caused us harm, we don't want forgiveness for them. We want justice! We wonder, "Why should I forgive them? They don't deserve it." You're right, they don't deserve it. Jesus acknowledges this with the debt of $20,000 in the story—not an insignificant amount. But when we don't forgive someone, we are keeping part of that person and the pain they caused us in our hearts. It is like stepping on glass and not cleaning out the cut, or taking the glass out of our foot. It stays in there and continues to cause pain and infections.

The Bible says those who don't forgive will be in torment. Consider all the ways that people are often in torment today. Which manifests itself through anxiety, depression, physical pain, and a host of other psychological and physical conditions. There are many possible reasons for these things, but one common reason is a wound from their past they still holding onto by not forgiving the perpetrator. It is like the piece of glass in their foot which keeps festering.

One of the greatest miracles God does for us is to help us forgive someone who has hurt us in the past. If the wound is serious, this isn't something we can do on our own. When we ask God to help us, He can change our hearts and give us the power to forgive. Colossians 3:13 admonishes us to,

"Bear with each other and forgive one another if any of you has a grievance against someone. Forgive as the Lord forgave you." (NIV)

pg. 158

None of this is easy. In fact, none of this is even possible without God's grace! Learning to make time for people, to listen well, to show up authentically, to serve unselfishly and to forgive lavishly can only be done by the power of God. I challenge you to seek His power each morning, deepen your friendship with Him, and then allow Him to teach you how to transform every other relationship.

Chapter Seven

Pillars of Physical Health

I was blessed with good genes and parents who raised me with healthy habits. Before my rock-climbing accident, I enjoyed great health without needing much effort or self-discipline. Health is one of those things that you don't think too much about until you have a problem. After my accident I was not allowed to put any weight on my left leg for three months. Since I also had broken my left arm, I wasn't able to walk more than a few feet even using my modified walker. I was basically bed ridden during this time.

After those three months I began slowly being able to put a little weight on my leg with the help of a walker, but it was still a long road to recovery. Two and half years after my accident I still couldn't walk properly and had to go back for a third surgery to have my hip completely replaced. I gained over 40 pounds during this time period and lost a lot of the energy, strength and vitality I once had.

I determined that I wasn't going to stay in that place however. I set out to discover what the secrets are to good health. As I researched and discovered I realized that many of these "secrets" are thing that I have known all along but hadn't paid that close of attention to because I was already enjoying great health.

The Bible reveals many secrets for enjoying physical health and long life. Some are no doubt thinking, *"Eat healthy, exercise, don't smoke or abuse alcohol and drugs— duh! That's not a secret."* Those things are important and the Bible gives us some specific advice along those lines, but what if I said the single most important factor affecting our life expectancy and our health isn't on this list? The latest research says that's the case, and the Bible has some great insights about it. Let's look at what God's ideal is for our physical health.

Let's start at the beginning. When God created Adam and Eve, His intention was that they would never die. There'd be no sickness, disease, or pain. Those things came about because of sin. Even after sin entered the world, people were still so physically strong and healthy that their life expectancy was over six hundred years. Let's consider life in the Garden of Eden. We'll discover seven pillars of physical health there that we can apply to our lives today.

If you read through the creation account in Genesis Chapter 1, you notice each day it says the evening and the morning were the (#) day. In God's design, the day starts in the evening. The evening is the time for rest, and the day is the time for work. God intended humans would work from their rest, not rest from their work. Adam and Eve's first day on earth was the Sabbath day. Before they'd ever done anything, they had an entire day of rest.

This is an important distinction because when we rest from our work, we're always depleting ourselves and then struggling to find the time to be rejuvenated. When we work from our rest, we're always full of God's strength and simply work from the overflow. That's because God's rest isn't just ceasing from activity, it involves entering into an experience of God himself which refreshes our soul. **God's Rest is our first pillar of physical health.** His rest is a supernatural experience which renews our hearts, souls, minds and bodies. This is why Hebrew 4:9-11 says,

> *"There remains, then, a Sabbath-rest for the people of God; for anyone who enters God's rest also rests from their works, just as God did from his. Let us, therefore, make every effort to enter that rest, so that no one will perish by following their example of disobedience." (NIV)*

Dr. Walter Cannon, a physiologist at Harvard University, performed an experiment studying a cat's vital functions when confronted by a dog.[iii] He noted the cat's circulation increased, its blood sugar levels increased, blood-clotting sped up, muscle functions increased, breathing quickened, senses became sharper, and unneeded digestive system functions stopped working.

These involuntary reactions increased cat's chances of surviving. The cat didn't think, "*Oh no, I better speed up my circulation and start breathing faster*"—it's the way God engineered the cat to react to a potential threat. All the changes prepared the cat to either fight or run away. This same thing happens to us.

When we experience an emergency, our bodies respond like the cat. Most of us don't arch our backs, expose our toenails, and hiss—although I am pretty sure I have seen some people do those things! All the other changes the experiment talked about happen inside us every time we perceive an emergency.

What would happen if the cat had those responses ten hours a day—for years? And what if the cat never actually fought or ran? I am pretty sure the cat would be so high-strung it would use up several of its nine lives. Some people have so much stress and anxiety they feel like they're constantly being chased by a Rottweiler. Imagine what this does to a body?

During the U.S. Civil War, they documented a severe anxiety condition called "soldier's heart." During World War I, they called it "shell shock." In World War II they termed it "battle fatigue." By the Vietnam War psychologists had termed it "post-traumatic stress disorder" (PTSD). Whatever we call it, it's caused by a constant "fight or flight" environment. Good thing we aren't in a war... oops, I almost forgot 1 Peter 2:11 reminds us,

"Dear friends, I urge you, as foreigners and exiles, to abstain from sinful desires, which wage war against your soul."

Your soul is at war. Some people believe that war is a metaphor for those desires tempting you to sin. But, one of the best definitions for sin I've heard is "trying to get your legitimate needs met from anywhere but God". Even good things can be sin if we're depending on them instead of God. If we rely on a human relationship to give us our identity, that becomes an idol, and it wars against our soul. If I rely on my job to take care of me instead of trusting God, that's sin, and it wars against my soul. God is the only thing we can't lose. So, when we depend on other things, we get pulled into never-ending battles with finances, job pressures, and family problems. We're at war, and those prolonged stress responses can wreak havoc with our immune system.

Stress is a major contributor to coronary heart disease, cancer, strokes, lung ailments, and accidental injuries—five of the leading causes of death in modern societies.

How can we escape this battle and leave stress behind? 2 Corinthians 10:3-5 gives us some insight,

> *"For though we live in the world, we do not wage war as the world does. The weapons we fight with are not the weapons of the world. On the contrary, they have divine power to demolish strongholds. We demolish arguments and every pretension that sets itself up against the knowledge of God, and we take captive every thought to make it obedient to Christ." (NIV)*

This text tells us we don't wage war the way the world does. Which begs the question: how does the world fight the everyday battles we face? It does it by striving, self-promoting, worrying, and relentless effort. So how do we fight? By trusting God's power, and resting in Him. Psalm 37:7-9 encourages us to,

"Rest in the LORD, and wait patiently for Him;

Do not fret because of him who prospers in his way,

Because of the man who brings wicked schemes to

pass.

Cease from anger, and forsake wrath;

Do not fret—it only causes harm.

For evildoers shall be cut off;

But those who wait on the LORD,

They shall inherit the earth." (NKJV)

God wants us to rest in Him. Not only by slowing down and relaxing, but by entering His presence and trusting Him. As 1 Peter 5:7 says,

"Cast all your anxieties upon Him, for He cares about you." (RSV)

Eden teaches us we need God's rest. What else can we learn from the garden? Let's move on to **the second pillar of health: Connecting with Nature.** Imagine what Eden looked like. Everything was freshly created. There was nothing dead anywhere. In fact, death was a concept Adam and Eve didn't really even understand. Eden was a garden God Himself planted. I've been in some beautiful gardens. I've toured the grounds at Buckingham Palace, and visited the famous botanical gardens in Victoria, British Columbia. But none of them compared to the beauty of the garden God made for Adam and Eve, and it was their home. They breathed the purest air, drank the purest water, and basked in the sunlight. Genesis 2:25 also tells us,

> *"They were both naked, the man and his wife, and were not ashamed." (NIV)*

I advise we try to live as close to the *"Eden"* lifestyle as possible, but I'm not advocating for nudity. Why? Because when sin entered, it became shameful to be naked. (Plus, there isn't enough bug spray and sunblock in the world to protect you if you were outside all day on hot days and you would freeze your tail off on wintry days!)

The point is Adam and Eve were one with nature. They existed in a natural setting all the time.

Imagine living in a beautiful garden. Nature wonderfully affects our mind. Scientists have discovered that experiencing nature is an important component of psychological well-being.

A University of Michigan research project found the pressures of modern life contribute to the experience of mental fatigue, which can lead to less tolerance, less effectiveness, and poorer health.[iv] By providing deeply needed restorative experiences, natural settings can play a central role in reducing those devastating effects.

If you're stressed, just soak in the beauties of nature. Studies find simply looking at a garden, the ocean, or a beautiful mountain can quickly reduce blood pressure and pulse rate and increases the brain activity that uplifts our mood.[v] In fact, when I was in the hospital for surgery recently my pulse was racing extremely high. The Doctor was first concerned and then amazed as my pulse dropped to a normal level within seconds. How? I visualized walking with Jesus in nature.

Researchers found the average anxiety level of individuals working in a building with plants to be lower than that of individuals working without plants. The research also showed the amount of sunlight also has a significant effect on job satisfaction. Having a view of natural elements actually makes it less likely for an employee to quit his or her job.[vi]

In her book Packing for Mars: The curious science of life in the void (2010), Mary Roach examines the effects of being disconnected from the earth.

"I once met a man who told me that after landing in Christchurch, New Zealand, after a winter at the South Pole research station, he and his companions spent a couple days just wandering around staring in

*awe at flowers and trees. At one point, one of them
spotted a woman pushing a stroller. 'A baby!' he
shouted, and they all rushed across the street to see.
The woman turned the stroller and ran."*

After months surrounded by frozen barrenness, the
simple sights of nature amazed the men. Roach explains
how an unnatural environment creates in all of us a
longing to return to nature. Mary continues,

*"Nothing tops space as a barren, unnatural
environment. Astronauts who had no prior interest in
gardening spend hours tending experimental
greenhouses. "They are our love," said cosmonaut
Vladislav Volkov of the tiny flax plants with which
they shared the confines of Salyut 1, the first Soviet
space station. She says, 'Humans don't belong in
space... Weightlessness is an exhilarating novelty, but
floaters soon begin to dream of walking.'* Earlier
[Alexandr] Laveikin told us, *'Only in space do you*

understand what incredible happiness it is just to walk. To walk on Earth.'"[vii]

Why is nature such a big deal for health? I believe it's because nature connects us back to God. God is the source of all life and He has placed that spark of connection into all His creation. When we encounter nature, we also end up encountering Him, and it renews our spirits. The following texts illustrate this:

Romans 1:20

> *"For since the creation of the world God's invisible qualities—his eternal power and divine nature—have been clearly seen, being understood from what has been made, so that people are without excuse." (NIV)*

Psalm 19:1

> *"The heavens declare the glory of God; the skies proclaim the work of his hands." (NIV)*

Job 12:7-9

> *"But ask the animals, and they will teach you, or the birds in the sky, and they will tell you; or speak to the earth, and it will teach you, or let the fish in the sea inform you. Which of all these does not know that the hand of the Lord has done this?* (NIV)

Nature is one of our primary connections to God. God is the source of all life, so it would make sense that whatever connects us back to Him will increase our health and vitality.

Exercise is our third pillar of physical health. There weren't cars in Eden, or anywhere in the Bible. Most people walked to their destinations, and their work was usually physical. Needing to worry about getting exercise is a pretty modern problem. The Bible doesn't say much about exercise because it wasn't an issue until the last hundred years or so. But this doesn't mean it isn't important. Jesus is our example, and He walked a lot. He didn't carry a pedometer, but I'm confident He was getting in way more than His 10,000 steps a day. In fact, scholars estimate that when He was traveling, *Jesus walked on average 25 miles a day,* so He had to be in good physical shape!

Now that I've given the mandatory encouragement to exercise, let's move on to the fourth pillar of physical health. **The fourth pillar is Trusting God.** Adam and Eve enjoyed easy and open communication with God. In fact, God came and walked with them through the garden each evening. Everything was great as long as they trusted Him. A lack of belief in what God told them led to their eating the fruit. All the brokenness in our world and our lives flows from not trusting God. But the good news is as we learn to trust Him, restoration and healing also begin to flow.

A May 2001 *Reader's Digest* article titled, "Why Doctors Now Believe Faith Heals," cited several studies by such reputable institutions as Duke University and

Dartmouth Medical School that link belief and personal health. Among the findings,

- *Those who attended religious services more than once a week enjoyed a seven-year-longer life expectancy than those who never attended.*
- *Older adults who considered themselves religious functioned better and had fewer problems than the nonreligious.*
- *Patients comforted by their faith were three times more likely to be living six months after open-heart surgery than those who found no emotional support in religion.*

The research seems to show the more spiritually committed you are, the more you benefit. Dr. Larry Dossey has written several books about the benefits of prayer and spirituality for healing. If you're interested in learning more on the subject the link to his website can be found in the endnotes.[viii] The medical community has a growing respect for the role faith and prayer play in our overall well-being.

It's interesting to me that when Jesus healed people He often said, "*Your faith has made you well,*" as He does in this passage from Luke 8:48,

> *And He said to her, "Daughter, be of good cheer; your faith has made you well. Go in peace." (NIV)*

Obviously it was His power that healed them, but I think what Jesus was saying is our faith and trust in Him is the key which unlocks His power and allows it to flow in our lives. This doesn't mean that if we pray and aren't healed, it's because of a lack of faith. There are many reasons our prayers sometimes aren't answered the way we desire, but those reasons are outside the scope of this book. Just understand faith is a necessary ingredient for miraculous healing, but it can't be assumed to *be* the problem if healing doesn't happen.

This brings us to the fifth pillar of health: **strong interpersonal relationships**. This pillar is the most important indicator of our physical health and life expectancy. The lack of this pillar in your life is more detrimental than smoking a pack of cigarettes a day. After God created Adam, He said,

> *"It is not good for the man to be alone. I will make a helper suitable for him." Genesis 2:18 (NIV)*

This is the only time God looked at something He'd made and said it wasn't good. Why? Because God made Adam in His image and God exists in community. God designed us to live in community.

We need other people in our life. Dr. Dean Ornish, in his book <u>Love and Survival: The Scientific Basis for the Healing Power of Intimacy,</u> writes,

> *"I'm not aware of any other factor in medicine—not diet, not smoking, not exercise, not stress, not genetics, not drugs, not surgery—that has a greater*

impact on our quality of life, incidence of illness, and the premature death from all causes than does love and intimacy." [ix]

When we say we need each other, it's more than just pleasant sounding words. God has created us for relationship, and when we don't have those connections, it's literally killing us.

The Complete Guide to Your Emotions and Your Health, published by Prevention Magazine, says,

"It seems something deep inside our cells responds positively when we feel love. Love appears capable of sparking healthy biological reactions in much the same way as good food and fitness." [x]

I'm not just talking about finding a good spouse and keeping that relationship healthy. A spouse is a glorious thing, but the research on longevity shows having **many** interpersonal relationships is the key factor in enjoying a long life.

The link between great relationships and physical health is very strong. In fact, scientists have a name for it—the Rosetto Effect. The name comes from a study spanning 50 years in the little town of Rosetto, Pennsylvania. Researchers discovered the incidence of coronary heart disease in Rosetto was about half of the two neighboring towns, despite the same risk factors in all three locations.

What was the difference? Rosetto was settled by a tightly knit group of religious immigrants from southern Italy. During the first 30 years of the study, they had a high level of social interaction: the entire community was like an extended family. They took care of each other and made sure nobody was ever lonely. The researchers thought this family-like atmosphere might protect the residents from heart disease and premature death. They showed their hypothesis to be true when, in the 1960s and

1970s, people started building bigger houses further away from each other and the community weakened. Sure enough, the heart disease rates in Rosetto climbed to the same levels as those in the other two communities.[xi]

I could quote numerous studies and statistics showing the importance of relationships for our health. When we have health, we take it for granted, but when we lose it we'd give up any amount of money to get it back. How sad it is that some people spend their lives pursuing riches and ruin both their relationships and their health. Then they end up spending all their money on healthcare. Even worse, many have sacrificed their relationship with God. Jesus said it this way,

> *"And what do you benefit if you gain the whole world but lose your own soul?"* Matthew 16:26 (NLT)

The sixth pillar of health is our Attitude. You may think, *"Wait a minute! I don't remember anything about that* *in the creation story."* Well, let's look again. Genesis 2:19 describes what happened after God created the animals.

> *"Out of the ground the Lord God formed every beast of the field and every bird of the air, and brought them to Adam". (NKJV)*

Try to picture this in your head. Presumably in that group of animals were saber-tooth tigers, woolly mammoths, dinosaurs, and crocodiles. Adam was basically in Jurassic park. But since there was no sin, the animals were tame and perfectly safe. Still, seeing such enormous animals could have been scary. Look what God did.

> [He] *"brought them to Adam to see what he would call them. And whatever Adam called each living creature, that was its name. So Adam gave names to all cattle, to the birds of the air, and to every beast of the field." (Genesis 2:19,20, NKJV)*

God was saying, "*Don't be afraid. These are your pets*" Adam had a whole zoo to play with!

From the beginning, God is helping Adam have a positive outlook. He didn't see dangers or enemies—he saw playmates. A few verses earlier in Genesis 2:8 it says,

> *"The Lord God planted a garden eastward in Eden, and there He put the man whom He had formed"* *(NKJV).*

God put Adam in a garden. He was helping Adam see the world as a safe place.

In the Garden of Eden, the first human being received a wonderful message—enjoy your life, you're safe, you're loved. Unfortunately, sin came in and shattered this perception. However, God has a provided a way back for us.

> *"And God raised us up with Christ and seated us with him in the heavenly realms in Christ Jesus."* *Ephesians 2:6 (NIV)*

That is our current reality! We can enjoy our life, we're safe, and we're loved. It's necessary to grab onto those thoughts and choose to live by that higher reality rather than believing in what we see around us. It's all about our attitude.

There's still **one pillar left** to cover, and you've probably already guessed it: **a Healthy Diet.** In Eden, God gave Adam and Eve the perfect diet. Genesis 1:29-30 reads,

> *"Then God said, 'I give you every seed-bearing plant on the face of the whole earth and every tree that has fruit with seed in it. They will be yours for food.'" (NIV)*

I want you to notice what's not on the list — vegetables. They're listed in the next verse,

> *"And to all the beasts of the earth and all the birds in the sky and all the creatures that move along the ground—everything that has the breath of life in it—I give every green plant for food."*

Vegetables were meant to be animal food. The original human diet was just fruits, grains, and nuts. Of course, meat and dairy weren't on the list either. God added those things after the flood because food was scarce, and perhaps less nutrient rich. So, I can't say never eat vegetables, meat, or dairy. If I did, I'd be a hypocrite. Each person is unique and must find the diet that works for them. But including a lot of fruits, vegetables, grains, and nuts is an excellent place to start. Also, even after the flood, God distinguished between clean and unclean animals. He gave only the clean animals as food. God didn't just arbitrarily decide to not allow His people to eat certain animals because He liked one kind over another. He knew eating some animals would be worse for your body than others. In the New Testament, God took away that restriction—not because the animals had suddenly become healthy to eat, but because the clean and unclean laws had turned into a barrier between Jews and Gentiles.

God wanted nothing to stand in the way of the gospel going to the gentile world.

It seems like every month a new diet plan comes and with new research to support it. These studies and plans seem to contradict each other, and it's confusing to figure out exactly what a healthy diet is. I find it helpful to use the Bible as my guide to help me cut through all the junk that's out there. After all, God is the one who made my body so it would make sense that He would know the best way to take care of it. Exodus 15:6 says,

> *"If you listen carefully to the Lord your God and do what is right in his eyes, if you pay attention to his commands and keep all his decrees, I will not bring on you any of the diseases I brought on the Egyptians, for I am the Lord, who heals you." (NIV)*

God actually promised that if we follow His guidelines, it would keep diseases away from us.

I don't want to give you hard and fast rules about what to eat. Instead, I think it's helpful to put things on a scale from most healthy to least healthy. Based on science and my reading of scripture, my list going from unhealthy to healthy would be: Poison, illegal drugs, nicotine, unclean meats, alcohol, processed grains, clean meats, dairy products, vegetables, whole grains, nuts, seeds, fruits.

Somewhere on that line you want to put a point where you won't ever eat anything toward the least healthy side. For example, most people would agree rat poison, Tide pods, and crack cocaine should be on the 'never' side of the point. Personally, I also put all unclean meats, such as pork and seafood, as well as alcohol and nicotine on the 'never' side. It's not that I think those things are sins, I'm simply convinced they'd be detrimental to my health. Everyone needs to decide where on this continuum they put their point. The Bible is helpful for organizing how healthy or unhealthy things are, but God gives us the freedom to choose.

The first step is to determine what goes in the 'never' category, then we must decide what should go in the 'seldom' category, the 'moderation' category and the 'as much as possible' category. In case you're interested, my personal classification is for 'seldom' on the clean meats and processed grains, 'moderation' on the dairy products and nuts, and 'as many as possible' for fruits, vegetables and seeds.

This chapter has shown what the ingredients are for good health, (the seven pillars) but it hasn't really explained how to implement them. I cover many of the pillars in other chapters, as health is interconnected with other aspects of our life. You read about how to have healthy relationships in the previous chapter, and how to have a positive attitude in chapter five. You will read in more detail about trusting God in the chapters coming on spirituality. I'm dedicating the last chapter of this book to helping you learn how to implement all the things I covered both in this chapter and the other portions of the book.

Chapter 8

Multiply Your Finances

I grew up in a family that by the world's standards would be considered very poor. We went through times when my mom wasn't working and my dad was pastoring a church as a volunteer, so we had absolutely no money coming in. At one point we lived in a house that was 25 feet x 25 feet and was over a hundred years old. It'd been vacant for several years before we moved in, and all the windows were broken. The house was standing because the termites were holding hands! There was no carpet and the plywood floor was rotting. My dad found a carpet store that was going out of business and got old carpet samples and carpeted the house with them. It looked like a patchwork quilt, but it was great for hopscotch. The kitchen cabinets had all rotted and were unusable, so my dad salvaged metal cabinets from a house that burned down and put them up in the kitchen. The city condemned the house when we moved out and had it torn down. However, as a child I never thought we were poor. I remember those days with fondness. They were some of the happiest of my life. The truth was my mother had offers all the time for her to earn good money as a nurse. There was a nursing shortage and since she had a degree in nursing, she was in high demand. But my family understood that true wealth is about more than money, and she felt her calling was to be at home being a mother to her sons.

God worked many miracles in those years in order to provide for our family. My dad would often open his Bible and money would fall out. When our car broke down and we needed a new one, we didn't tell anyone, we just prayed. Shortly after that, someone gave my dad a check for $500. He put it in his pocket and when he pulled it out later it was a check for $5000. This was in the late 1970s when $5000 would buy a pretty nice used car. (I've always wondered if God put the corresponding amount into the person's bank account, or if He just let them know they needed to be even more generous.)

I shared this story because I want to make a few things clear at the outset. First, Philippians 4:19 promises,

> *"God will meet all your needs according to His glorious riches in Christ Jesus." (NIV)*

God has promised to take care of all our needs, but not necessarily all our wants. Just like any good parent, He doesn't always give His children everything they ask for because He knows it isn't ultimately the best thing for them.

Second, it's important to understand that true wealth is about much more than just money. Third, God wants us to have financial security which doesn't mean what the world thinks it means. Having a lot of money isn't financial security, it's actually financial insecurity because it can always be lost. True financial security comes from relying on God and not on money to take care of us. If we rely on money rather than God to take care of us it becomes a curse rather than a blessing. The more money you have the harder it is not to begin trusting in it. That is why Jesus said blessed are the poor. The poor have any easier time trusting in God because they don't have any money to rely on instead.

Money can be a useful tool to accomplish much good but it can also easily ruin your life. Therefore God only entrusts wealth to those who will see themselves as stewards of that wealth and not allow it to capture there hearts. There are some character traits that we need to demonstrate before God can trust us with financial resources that might cause us great harm. One of the character traits we most need is a love for God that is so passionate that it leaves no room for loving money. Another character trait that God is looking for is generosity. God Himself is a generous God and He loves it when His children follow His example.

One scripture most people would love to see manifest in their lives is Proverbs 10:22 which says,

"The blessing of the Lord brings wealth, without painful toil for it." (NIV)

This sounds like the best get rich quick scheme ever. Simply get God's blessing and you'll be wealthy without all the painful toil. However, there are three questions we need to answer if we're going to experience this.

1. How do we get the God's blessing?
2. What is meant by wealth?
3. What does it mean to get wealth without painful toil?

So, how do we get God's blessing on our life? Deuteronomy 28:2 tell us,

"All these blessings will come on you and accompany you if you obey the Lord your God." (NIV)

The entire chapter of Deuteronomy 28 lays out all the blessings that come from obedience and the curses that come from disobedience. It's the premise of this book that all of God's laws are not arbitrary but descriptive. It's part of the design. God is not rewarding your obedience, rather, when we live our lives in line with the principles He set up, the blessing is automatically unlocked.

However, because of the power of sin operating in our lives, we couldn't live in harmony with those principles, so Jesus came to deliver us from the power of sin. He took the curses on Himself, and He broke sin's power. He gave us grace, so we now have the power to live in harmony with God's principles and reap the blessings.

What are the Biblical conditions we must meet in order to unlock the financial blessing that God has for us?

There are many financial principles of saving, spending, giving, investing, and using our resources throughout the Bible. Let's look specifically at six.

1. We have to ask for His help.

James 4:2 tells us,

"*You do not have because you do not ask God.*" (NIV)

God wants us to ask Him for things. It gives Him an opportunity to show His love to us. But most of us just buy what we need. I want to challenge you to start asking God for the things you want and give Him the chance to bring it to you. Some of us are okay asking God for our needs, but asking for our wants feels selfish, like we shouldn't bother God with such frivolous things. But God loves us and wants good things for us. That doesn't mean He'll always say yes, but sometimes He will and He loves it when we ask. I've had the experience many times of asking God for something I desired and then finding it that very day on the street corner, or other times, someone calls me up and asks me if I could use the very item I asked God for. It doesn't always happen; many times I don't get what I want, but when I do it is extra special because the item reminds me of God's love and care for me.

In Matthew 7:7 Jesus says,

"Ask and it will be given you. Search, and you will find. Knock, and the door will open for you." (NIV)

and in John 16:24,

"Until now you have asked for nothing in My name; ask and you will receive, so that your joy may be made full." (NASB)

The key part of this verse is asking in Jesus' name. That means asking on His behalf. In other words, we're asking for God's purposes, and not our own selfish interest. When we do this, it makes our joy full. When we see God's work in and through our lives, it releases great joy in our hearts.

2. We need to be content with what we have.

1 Timothy 6:6 says,

"Yet true godliness with contentment is itself great wealth." **(NLT)**

In the context this verse is a warning against those who try to use Biblical principles to get rich without caring about their relationship with God or their own character development. It is a reminder that true wealth is more than just money, and that contentment is a necessary ingredient in that true wealth. Contentment doesn't mean that we don't have any dreams or goals. We can, and should have goals, even financial goals.

Contentment means that we don't rely on stuff to make us happy. It's an attitude that says, *"God is all I need, and I'll be happy even if God is all I ever have."* It's recognizing that our circumstances won't bring us happiness, and instead look to God to bring us fulfillment. Paul learned contentment. In Philippians 4:12 he said,

> "*I know how to live on almost nothing or with everything. I have learned the secret of living in every situation, whether it is with a full stomach or empty, with plenty or little.*" (NLT)

Contentment is something we have to learn. It's not something that comes naturally. He wants us to ask when we have a need and learn to be content, that our happiness isn't dependent on how much or how little we've got. If we don't learn contentment, we'll never be happy because we'll always want more.

In this verse Paul doesn't actually tell us what the secret is to being content, but I think He had already spilled the beans a few chapters earlier. In Philippians 2:14 he admonished,

"Do everything without complaining

and arguing." (NLT)

The way we learn contentment is by practicing doing everything without complaining and instead *"give thanks in all circumstances,"* 1 Thessalonians 5:18 (NIV).

3. We must give in faith.

2 Corinthians 9:6-7 advises us,

"Remember this, whoever sows sparingly will also reap sparingly. And whoever sows generously will also reap generously. Each one should give what he has decided in his heart to give, not reluctantly or under compulsion for God loves a cheerful giver." (NIV)

Don't give because you feel pressured to give. If you get one of those phone calls where people are twisting your arm to donate and you start to feel resentful, don't give to them. Give when you can do it joyfully, knowing that God will give back much more than you give away.

2 Corinthians 9:8 says,

> "*And God is able to make all grace abound to you, so that always having all sufficiency in everything, you may have an abundance for every good deed.*" *(NASB)*

This is the principle of Sowing and Reaping. This principle is one of those universal laws from a previous chapter. If we sow criticism, we'll reap criticism. If we sow kindness, we'll reap kindness. If we sow generosity, it's going to come back to us and we'll reap generosity. Whatever we need more of, we give away.

This principle is so well known that people have abused it. I've heard people say "*Sow $10,000 into my ministry and God will bring you back a million.*" That's manipulation, and not how it works. You sow by using your resources the way God tells you to, not the way some preacher on TV says. Also, you may sow money, but the harvest may come in things that are much more valuable than money. But just because the principle has been abused doesn't mean it isn't true. Every farmer knows this principle works. They don't expect things to grow in a field they haven't planted. They know if they expect a harvest, they have to plant what they want to grow. They don't say, "I've only a little of this corn left so I can't afford to sow it." If they sow that corn, they know they'll get back much more corn than they sow. In Luke 6:38 Jesus said,

> "*Give and it will be given unto you. And the measure you use to give out will be the measure which God uses to give back to you.*" (NIV)

God wants us to be givers because He is a giver. He wants us to learn to be just like Him. He is trying to develop in us the character trait of generosity.

We think, "*When all my needs are met, then I'll give.*" God says, "*No, when you give, then all your needs will be* met." God wants us to give things away even when we feel we can't afford it, because doing so demonstrates our faith and trust in Him to take care of us.

Proverbs 3:9-10 says,

> Honor the Lord with your wealth, with the first-fruits of all your crops; then your barns will be filled to overflowing, and your vats will brim over with new wine... (NIV)

This text tells us to give God the first part of our income. The Bible calls this tithe (the first ten percent). Tithing isn't giving. Tithing is an act of faith and worship. We're returning a portion to God as way of saying, "You own all of it and I trust You to take care of me. I won't trust in money, or my job, or another person. I trust You to take care of me." God doesn't need our money. He paved the streets in heaven with gold. He can speak into existence anything He wants. So why does He ask us to return tithe to Him? Because He wants our hearts. He knows that money can easily move in and take over our hearts. Tithing is a way of keeping money in its proper place and keeping God on the throne. Jesus tells us in Matthew 6:21 that,

> "*where your treasure is*
> *there your heart will be also.*" (NIV)

If we say Jesus is number one in our life, but He's not first in our finances and our time, He's not first. We need to quit kidding ourselves.

Give the first part of the income to the Lord and watch Him bless it. It's similar to setting aside part of each day as a quiet time with the Lord and seeing Him make the rest of the day expand so we can get more done. When we give the first 10% of our income to the Lord, somehow He makes that other 90% expand so we can pay more with what remains.

4. We must maintain our integrity.

God doesn't bless dishonesty. Proverbs 16:11,

"The Lord demands fairness in
every business deal." (TLB)

That includes wages, sales, even taxes. If we want God's blessing on our finances, we've got to be honest. We can't rip people off. Proverbs 28:6 advises,

"Better to be poor and honest than rich and
dishonest." (GNT)

Why? Because Jesus said in Mark 8:36,

"What does it profit a man if he gains the whole world
and loses his soul?" (KJV)

We'll always reap what we sow. If we're dishonest with others, dishonesty will be returned to us. Be honest with your finances. If you run a business, do it with integrity. As I was writing this chapter, I started thinking about my friend Jim, who works in the sales industry. Having done sales myself, I know the industry is ultimately focused on money and making sales goals. Jim refuses to focus on sales however and instead looks for ways that he can serve his clients. He begins each day by asking God where He wants him to go and then does what God says. When he became the top salesperson for his company in the southeastern United States, the CEO sent someone down to learn how he did it.

The big wig sat in Jim's car and said, "*Where are we going?*" Jim said, "*I don't know yet I'm waiting for God to tell me.*" They waited for about 10 minutes before Jim got a sense of where God wanted him to go. The executive was growing increasingly impatient. The company sold chemical supplies to hotels. Jim was impressed to go to a particular hotel the company had pursued for years, but they hadn't made a single sale, as the hotel was very loyal to their competitor. When the company man heard where

Jim was headed he got upset. He said, "*You're wasting our time, they're never going to buy from us. You're just stringing me along. This isn't how you make sales. Show me what you really do.*" Jim insisted they were going to go to that hotel.

When they walked in the door, the hotel manager saw him and said, "*I'm so glad you're here! I'm so mad right now. My pool is a mess, the chemicals are all out of whack, and the chemical supply company we use said they can't get me what I need for four more days. If you can get my pool straightened out, I'll switch all of our accounts over to you.*" My friend Jim met his sales goals for the entire quarter in that one visit, and the guy from his company had to pick his jaw up off the floor. That is what it means to maintain your integrity and to receive the blessings of God.

5. We must trust Him with our lives.

In Matthew chapter 6, Jesus is encouraging us not to worry about money or how we will get the things we need to survive. In verse 31-33 He says,

> "*So don't worry about these things, saying, 'What will we eat? What will we drink? What will we wear?' These things dominate the thoughts of unbelievers, but your heavenly Father already knows all your needs. Seek the Kingdom of God above all else, and live righteously, and he will give you everything you need.*" (NLT)

Everyone wants to have no financial worries, but most people have the mistaken belief that they need more money to achieve that. In reality, the more people possess, the more they worry about it. The real secret to losing all your financial worries is right here in Matthew 6, where we're told to trust God to supply all our needs, and then let Him worry about it.

When I was a kid, anytime I had a need I'd go to my parents and say, "*I'm hungry*", or "*I need new shoes.*" I never worried about money. It was my parents' job to take care of me, and I knew they would. I never stressed out worrying, "*What if we run out of food?*" But then I grew up, and sometimes I acted like a spiritual orphan. I'd sometimes forget that I've got a heavenly Father who promises to take care of everything. If we want to live worry-free lives, we have to become like little children and constantly remind ourselves that it isn't up to us. We've a heavenly Father who has promised to provide.

Humans are the only creatures that worry. Does your parakeet worry? No. Does your garden worry? No. We're the only organisms that worry. Everything else trusts God. The Bible says if God takes care of the birds, don't you think He'll take care of you if you trust Him? How much do we trust God?

When we worry, we become 'practical atheists'. We may claim to believe in God, but in practicality we act like it all depends on us instead of God. Worry is a signal to us that we aren't trusting God. It should cause us to turn immediately to God and ask Him to calm our hearts.

6. We must learn to live debt free.

Romans 5:8 instructs us to,

"owe nothing to anyone—except for your obligation to love one another." (NLT)

This principle is very important because as Proverbs 22:7 informs us,

"The borrower is slave to the lender." (NIV)

I don't want to be a slave to anything. I want to be free to do whatever God asks of me without reservation. Full disclosure: I'm not fully living in harmony with this principle. I still owe my mortgage, my student loans, the second mortgage we took out to pay for my daughter's adoption, and other miscellaneous debts. But I'm praying for more of God's grace in my life so I can learn to live in harmony with this principle and be completely free to follow the Spirit's lead in my life. If God asked me to quit my job and move to, say, India, I wouldn't be free to just go because I've all these debts I'm legally and morally obligated to pay.

At the beginning of this chapter, I quoted Proverbs 10:22. Let me remind you of it again.

> *"The blessing of the Lord brings wealth, without painful toil for it." (NIV)*

There were three questions we must answer to apply this verse to our lives. **First,** *how do we get God's blessing?* **I trust the six points above have answered that. So on to the second question.** *What is meant by wealth?* Luke 16:11 states,

"So if you have not been trustworthy in handling worldly wealth, who will trust you with true riches?" (NIV)

This text shows us that money isn't real wealth, but how we handle money determines if we can be trusted with true wealth.   The money we have isn't ours, we're managers. That is why the next verse says,

"And if you have not been trustworthy with someone else's property, who will give you property of your own?" Luke 16:12 (NIV)

The problem with money is that is can seduce our hearts. It can cause us to move our affections from God to money. 1 Timothy 6:10 says,

"For the love of money is a root of all kinds of evil. Some people, eager for money, have wandered from the faith and pierced themselves with many griefs." (NIV)

This verse is often misquoted. People often say, "Money is the root of all evil," but that isn't true. It's the **love** of money that's the root of evil, and often those who have the least love it the most.

If we can remember that we're only managing the money in our possession and always use it for God's purposes, then He may trust us with more money. The money He trusts us with isn't His blessing though; it is a responsibility. In fact, if we can't manage money well it can be a curse in our lives. That's why so many lottery winners actually end up feeling miserable. Don McNay, a financial consultant to lottery winners and author of the book **Life Lessons from the Lottery,** says of lottery winners, "*So many of them wind up unhappy or wind up broke. People have had terrible things happen.,*"[xii] That's why Jesus said, "*Blessed are the poor.*" (Luke 6:20 NIV) The poor don't have to contend with the curse that money can be in life.

So what does it mean to be blessed and have true wealth? Jesus statement that the poor are blessed is a big clue. The poor find it easy to depend on God to take care of them. The wealthy are often tempted to depend on themselves and their wealth. God warns against this Jeremiah 17:5-6,

> "This is what the Lord says, 'Cursed is the one who trusts in man, who depends on flesh for his strength and whose heart turns away from the Lord. He will be like a bush in the wastelands; he will not see prosperity when it comes. He will dwell in the parched places of the desert, in a salt land where no one lives.'" (NIV)

When we trust in money, we're trusting in man and that brings a curse on our life instead of a blessing. This is why 1 Timothy 6:17 tells us to

> "teach those who are rich in this world not to be proud and not to trust in their money, which is so unreliable. Their trust should be in God, who richly gives us all we need for our enjoyment." (NLT)

Money is unreliable. No matter how much we have, we can still lose it. But we can never lose God. He has promised to never leave us or forsake us.

A truly blessed and wealthy life comes from being in a right relationship with God. If we want to live with no worries, money isn't the answer. The more money we have, the more we have to worry about. But if we whole heartedly trust God, then we're like a child; we've no worries. Being in this childlike state is also what allows us to experience all the other blessings that God desires to bring. That is why the Bible says to,

> *"seek first the kingdom of God, and his righteousness; and all these things shall be added unto you."*
> *Matthew 6:33 (NIV)*

The third question was, *what does it mean to get wealth without painful toil?* Does this mean that since God is taking care of us, we don't need to work? This is an excellent question, in Matthew 6:24 Jesus says,

> "*No one can serve two masters. Either he will hate the one and love the other, or he will be devoted to the one and despise the other. You cannot serve both God and Money.*" (NIV)

If we're only working for money, then we're serving money and that is when toil is especially painful. Let me paraphrase this verse. "*You cannot work for two bosses. Either you will love one and hate the other, or you will secretly despise one and be totally devoted to the other. You can't work for both God and money.*" (That's my new Jemly paraphrase!) So, according to the Bible, a Christian answer as to why we work cannot be that we need money. A Christian doesn't need money. The Bible says we're to take no thought for it because we've a heavenly Father who takes care of all our needs.

We need a better reason to work. If not for money, why else would we work? Isn't that why most people dream of winning the lottery—so they can stop working? If we aren't working for money, then what's the point?

Genesis 2:15 gives us a clue. It says,

"The Lord God took the man and put him in the Garden of Eden to work it and take care of it." (NIV)

Before sin ever entered, God gave man work. He didn't give the work so Adam and Eve could get money. They didn't need money. There was no such thing as money. They didn't work to provide for their food. God had already planted the garden, they had everything they needed. God gave them work because work is a blessing. It's a way for us to be like God, who's always working and creating.

Notice God gave the work to Adam and Eve in the garden before there was sin. Work isn't a curse, it's a blessing! When sin entered the world, God pronounced a curse that made work more difficult, but work itself is still a blessing. Because Jesus died and provided a way back to God, the effects of sin are reversed the closer we come to God. So, the closer we get to God, the more we'll find that we enjoy work. It will be less hard and more of a blessing.

Work is a blessing so if by some miracle I won the lottery, (and it would be a miracle, because I don't play!) I wouldn't quit my job. No matter how much money I had, I would still keep doing what I'm doing. I don't work for money. I work for God. Some would say sure, that makes sense because you're a minister, but what if I'm just trying to get a paycheck so I can survive?

When we're just working to get a paycheck, we're working for money and need to change bosses. Now that doesn't mean that we have to change jobs. Check out Colossians 3:22-24.

"Slaves, obey your earthly masters in everything; and do it, not only when their eye is on you and to curry their favor, but with sincerity of heart and reverence for the Lord. Whatever you do, work at it with all your heart, as working for the Lord, not for human masters, since you know that you will receive an inheritance from the Lord as a reward. It is the Lord Christ you are serving." (NIV)

Paul is talking here to people who are caught in the terrible institution of slavery. People misused this verse to claim God condones slavery, but that's not the case. He is merely talking to people who find themselves caught in that situation and telling them how they should behave. Actually, he is telling them how they can find freedom.

Have you ever felt like a slave at work, like they don't pay you enough, they don't treat you well enough, but you feel stuck because you just don't have any other options? Paul is talking to actual slaves who didn't have the luxury of changing jobs, even if they wanted to, but he is telling them they can change bosses. We can have the attitude that says, "*I'm not doing this for the measly little paycheck that they're giving me. I'm doing this for the Lord.*" What that does is give us back the dignity and the pride of our work. Even for those who were actual slaves, they could decide they were now working for God and that their work had purpose. It doesn't matter if your boss appreciates you, it doesn't matter if other people notice what you do because you're working for God.

When we have this attitude, it frees us to enjoy our work. Our work will no longer be painful toil; it will be a blessing. When your boss is demanding and overbearing, you can just smile and think, "I don't work for you, my boss is a Jewish carpenter." Now, I don't recommend you say that out loud! But the point is, this attitude can free us from worrying about what people think about us, and whether we'll lose our job. Our provisions, what we need for our lives, don't come from our job, they come from

God. Because God has told us that if we seek Him, He will provide for all our needs.   He may choose to bring provisions to us through our job, but He may choose to bring it to us another way when we choose to work, not for the money, but to please God. God won't fire us! Even if we lose our current employment, He is simply transferring us to another position.

I want to point out what Solomon said about work. In Ecclesiastes 3:22 he said,

> *"So I saw that there is nothing better for a person than to enjoy their work, because that is their lot. For who can bring them to see what will happen after them?" (NIV)*

Solomon says that the best thing we can enjoy is work. It is better than ice cream, better than chocolate, better that sports, better than games, better than anything else that we enjoy.

This chapter is talking about work because so many of us depend on our jobs for security. God want us to trust Him with our lives because whenever we trust anything else, whether it's the money we have in the bank, our job, a relationship, or our education, it will become a source of anxiety for us because it can be taken away. Only when we're truly relying on God, can we live worry-free. Jesus said where your treasure is, there your heart will be also. However, I think it is just as valid to reverse it and say where your heart is there your treasure will be also. So, if you want to be truly financially free, set your heart on things above!

Chapter Nine

Finding Your Purpose

There was a time in my life when I felt like I had no purpose. The doorway to things I believed God had asked me to do seemed to be closed. I thought God was calling me into church planting, but all the doors had been shut. I was a struggling insurance salesman who was spending more on gas than I was making in commissions. It seemed like I would never have the chance to fulfill the dreams that God had placed in my heart. I finally came to the place where I told God that I was okay if it was His plan to "waste my life" doing things that made little sense to me. I would trust Him and be grateful and satisfied with my life.

Six months later, a pathway to my dreams opened in a much broader way than what I had expected. Though my plan had been to support myself as an insurance salesman while planting a church, God brought me a full-time paid position as a church planter. God is the one who had placed the church planting dream in my heart all along, but He had to teach me not to draw my identity and worth from what I do.

This has been a lifelong struggle for me. I have always been an overachiever, and drew my sense of self-worth from my accomplishments. However, because of the trials and experiences God has brought me through, I now find great freedom drawing my identity from Christ. I have nothing to prove; I am a child of the King of the Universe and I represent Him in this world. I still feel the pull of accomplishment, a desire for accolades, and a drive to prove what I am capable of. I have to constantly guard my heart and refocus my thoughts on how much God loves me. This helps me enjoy life and ironically, to accomplish more than I ever could by striving.

As I look around our world, I see people everywhere scratching, clawing, and hustling to achieve *something* so they can finally feel good about themselves. All their striving is chasing after the wind. The following anecdote illustrates the situation of so many in our world today. A man was in a hurry to catch his plane. He pushed his way through a crowd and ran for a taxi, he pushed aside an old lady that was slowly getting into one and jumped in. He yelled, "Go fast! I am in a hurry, there is a big tip in it for you if you drive fast." The driver floored it and took off. The man put his head in his hands, rubbed his eyes and tried to relax.

Ten minutes later he opened his eyes and glanced out the window and saw they were going in the wrong direction. Realizing he hadn't told the driver where to take him, he called out, "Do you know where you're going?" The driver replied, "No, but I am driving fast".

There are many people in our world who are like that. They are moving fast, but they don't know where they are going. They are going the wrong way because they don't understand what their purpose is. Imagine if I was a toolmaker, and I made hammers, saws, tape measures and similar tools. But let's imagine these tools were intelligent and capable of acting on their own, and the hammer decided its purpose was to cut things, and tried to act accordingly and the saw decided its purpose was to measure things —imagine a running chain saw coming at you to measure your inseam...yikes!

The one who makes something knows what it is for. He is the one who created it for a specific reason. It's ridiculous for a creation to tell the creator what its purpose is. Isaiah 29:15 puts it this way,

"You turn things upside down, as if the potter were thought to be like the clay! Shall what is formed say to the one who formed it, 'You did not make me'? Can the pot say to the potter, 'You know nothing'?" (NIV)

In case you have any doubt who the clay is in this text, Isaiah tells us explicitly in Isaiah 64:8. He says,

> "*Yet you, Lord, are our Father. We are the clay, you are the potter; we are all the work of your hand.*" (NIV)

Someone once said, "*There are two great days in a person's life — the day we are born and the day we discover why.*" God has placed within each of us a dream that gives us insight into what His purpose is for us. But sometimes life happens in such a way that the dream seems lost and everything seems to have gone horribly wrong. However, God's purpose for us has never changed; it is just different from what we imagined. Sadly, if we don't understand what our purpose is we will constantly feel like our life is a struggle because we will always be trying to work against what God is trying to do through us.

We must find our purpose in God. If anyone tries to find their purpose in any other relationship or activity, they are looking in the wrong place. Hebrews 9:27 warns us,

> "... *people are destined to die once, and after that to face judgment.*" (NIV)

The entire purpose of our lives is to prepare to stand before God. Our lives on earth are very short in the scheme of eternity, but what we do with them will determine what will happen to us for eternity. In Psalm 144:3-4 David said this,

> "*Lord, what are human beings that you care for them, mere mortals that you think of them? They are like a breath; their days are like a fleeting shadow.*" (NIV)

Our life here is just a breath. Take a moment to breathe in..... and exhale. That is how our life here will seem in eternity. Just a passing breath. The longer I'm alive, the more I realize how time really flies. We have little time to fulfill our purpose before we will stand before God for judgment.

We should focus all of our short time here on preparing for that moment. Some people comprehend this and so they try really hard to live a life that is good enough. But that is a losing battle as no one can ever live a life which measures up to God's standards. What a tragedy it would be to live our entire lives just trying to please God and then discover it was all in vain.

The good news is Jesus has already lived a perfect life, and by accepting Him as Lord and Savior we can stand before God and be judged on His merits. This is why Jesus is the only way we can reconnect to God, and to our purpose. In John 14:6 Jesus explicitly tells us,

> *"... I am the way and the truth and the life. No one comes to the Father except through me." (NIV)*

Most of us have probably heard this before and have already taken the step of praying a prayer accepting Jesus as Lord and Savior. However, accepting something intellectually and living it out aren't the same thing. Jesus said in Matthew 7:21-23 that many people who call Him Lord will be lost.

> *"Not everyone who says to me, 'Lord, Lord,' will enter the kingdom of heaven, but only the one who does the will of my Father who is in heaven. Many will say to me on that day, 'Lord, Lord, did we not prophesy in your name and in your name drive out demons and in your name perform many miracles?' Then I will tell them plainly, 'I never knew you. Away from me, you evildoers!'"* (NIV)

Some might think we are back to trying to work to please God. But let's look a little closer. Jesus says only those who do the will of the Father will enter the kingdom of heaven. He then lists many things which seem like they would be God's will, including driving out demons and performing miracles. But the condemnation comes from the fact they don't really know Jesus. According to John 17:3 eternal life comes from knowing Jesus and the Father. Which is informative, but what does it have to do with God's will? 2 Peter 3:9 gives us another piece of the puzzle, it says,

> *"The Lord is not slack concerning his promise, as some men count slackness; but is longsuffering to us-ward, not willing that any should perish, but that all should come to repentance." (NIV)*

If we put these two concepts together (eternal life comes from knowing God, and God's will is for everyone to have eternal life) it follows that it's God's will for you to know Him. So, not everyone who calls Jesus Lord will enter heaven, but only those who do the will of the Father—which is to know Him. This is why the condemnation given in Matthew 7:23 is,

> *"I never knew you." (NIV)*

2 Thessalonians 1:7-9 is another passage that tells us the same thing,

> "... This will happen when the Lord Jesus is revealed from heaven in blazing fire with his powerful angels. He will punish those who do not know God and do not obey the gospel of our Lord Jesus. They will be punished with everlasting destruction and shut out from the presence of the Lord and from the glory of His might." (NIV)

When Jesus returns, He will punish those who don't know God. It isn't as though God is being vengeful; He is simply giving people what they've chosen. They're being shut out from His presence. God allows everyone the opportunity to experience His goodness, but He allows those who choose not to engage with Him to walk away. Since God is the source of all life, separation from Him leads to destruction.

Our primary purpose in life is to know God. I have written a book titled <u>God's Submarines</u>[xiii] which is full of tools to help everyone deepen their relationships with Him. However, you don't have to read it to know God better. God promises if we seek Him we will find Him. Our number one quest is simply to seek God.

That being said, God has a special calling on my life, and yours. He has something specific for each of us to accomplish, but we must be careful that we don't confuse our "who" and our "do". Identity and purpose don't come from what we do. The entire purpose of life is to enjoy intimacy with God. Our identity flows out of our relationship to Him. If I were to ask, *"Who are you?"* many people would simply give me their name. But if I pushed back and said, *"No, who are you really?"* what response would I get? Some people might tell me their job. *"I am Doctor, I am an architect, etc."* Other would define themselves in terms of relationships. *"I am mother, a wife and a best friend."*

Stop and think for a minute. How would you answer the question "Who are you, really"? Any answer which doesn't flow from a relationship to God is based on something that can be destroyed. I have met plenty of people who get their identity from their work, for much of my life I was one of them. When I lost my job, I felt useless and lost my identity. I have met many other people who defined themselves as parents, and when their kids grew up and moved away, they felt lost and unneeded.

Once we have given control of our lives to God our true identity is *a child of God, a coheir with Christ, an Ambassador of the King of the Universe.* We find our purpose and identity in Him. This doesn't mean God has nothing for us to do, but the things we do will flow out of our identity as children of God and being part of the body of Christ. We do nothing to become a body part or a child of God. We will do lots of things **because** we are God's Ambassador and His servant, but never in order to become one. It's just like being a family member. Because I am part of my family, I do dishes and take out the trash and a million other things. I never once believed I had to do those things to get into the family, whether it was my family growing up or the family I formed with my wife. Yet, so many people try to do this very thing with God.

One truth which flows out of finding our identity in God is that we are God's ministers. God has called all Christians to be ministers. Every believer is just as much a minister of the gospel as is the pastor of their church. There is no difference between their callings. God sets people up as overseers of ministries. This is a position of authority and responsibility, but it doesn't mean the pastor of a church is holier than anyone else or has a more special calling on their life. We are each called to minister in our own unique sphere and way.

God has given grace to His people to minister for Him in five specific ways, to fight for his army in five specific spheres - as an apostle, prophet, evangelist, teacher or pastor.

Ephesians 4:7-13 tells us,

> *"But to each one of us grace has been given as Christ apportioned it. This is why it says, 'When he ascended on high, he took many captives and gave gifts to his people.' (What does 'he ascended' mean except that he also descended to the lower, earthly regions? He who descended is the very one who ascended higher than all the heavens, in order to fill the whole universe.) So Christ himself gave the apostles, the prophets, the evangelists, the pastors and teachers, to equip his people for works of service, so that the body of Christ may be built up until we all reach unity in the faith and in the knowledge of the Son of God and become mature, attaining to the whole measure of the fullness of Christ." (NIV)*

You may have heard these five gifts are special gifts God has given for the leaders of the church, and it sets aside people with these gifts from everyone else for a unique purpose. But that isn't true. Verse seven says God has given each one of us grace as Christ apportioned it. There is no mention of leadership anywhere in this verse! God has given each of us the grace to minister in some of these ways.

If anyone doesn't understand their calling, they need to discover it and begin pressing into it. They may have another job, but their full-time vocation is the ministry God has called them to. Paul had a job as a tentmaker. His provision came to him through that. We would say that was how he earned his living. But Paul didn't see himself as a tentmaker. Paul saw himself the way God saw him -- as an apostle. Because Paul agreed with God and acted accordingly, other people also recognized Paul as an apostle. The fivefold ministries are not a job God asks us to do. They are types of ministers He calls us to be.

One person's job may be nursing, another working at a grocery store selling cars, or anything else. That is fine, they should keep doing that as long as God keeps them there. But God calls each of us to be a minister. Ministry isn't something we do at a church. Ministry is something we do wherever we go. Because where ever we go the church is there. We are the church.

The fivefold ministry expresses the fullness of Christ's ministry. You will find all five ministry titles applied to Christ at various times in scripture. So for the church to have the fullness and stature of Christ as Ephesians talks about, we need to be operating in all five ways. As we individually become more like Jesus we should strive for and expect to minister in all five ways ourselves, but there will always be one or two areas we have a special anointing for. Why? Because God has given us the grace to be that type of minister. God designed that we would always need each other. It is only as each of us becomes mature and we work together that the fullness of Jesus' ministry is manifest. God knows that if any one of us could do everything that Jesus did, we would become proud and puffed up. We wouldn't be able to handle the praise and it would ultimately ruin us.

It's important to understand the fivefold ministry is not the same thing as spiritual gifts. Spiritual gifts are the tools God gives us to do ministry. Those tools are not necessarily permanent. God often gives us the gifts which are needed for the moment and when they are no longer needed, they go away. The fivefold ministry is permanent because it is what God gives you the grace to **be**.

The Bible says there also false ministers. How do you recognize the difference between true and false apostles, prophets, and other ministers, and how do you make sure you aren't a false one? Jesus said by their fruits

you shall know them. What are the fruits?
Galatians 5:22-23 tell us,

> *"But the fruit of the Spirit is love, joy,*
>
> *peace, forbearance, kindness, goodness,*
>
> *faithfulness, gentleness and self-control. Against such*
>
> *things there is no law." (NIV)*

Someone who is very gifted but doesn't
demonstrate the fruits of the Spirit is a false minister. To
minister means to serve. So, if someone claims to be a
minister of any kind but they are all about other people
serving them, and wanting titles, and position, they are a
false minister. A true minister is one who serves. Real
service is done from love, which is the first fruit of the
Spirit. Look at the example of Jesus in John 13:3-5,

> *"Jesus knew that the Father had put all things under*
>
> *his power, and that he had come from God and was*
>
> *returning to God; so he got up from the meal, took off*

his outer clothing, and wrapped a towel around his waist. After that, he poured water into a basin and began to wash his disciples' feet, drying them with the towel that was wrapped around him." (NIV)

Jesus knew He had all authority, so He served. This is what it means to be a minister. We are all called to serve, but the way we serve is unique and will flow through one or two of the aspects of the fivefold ministry.[3]

Pastors are the shepherds, and it is unfortunate we call the overseer of a church the pastor because it has made it hard for people to see themselves as a pastor when in fact it is probably the most common ministry function in the church. This is because it is the most needed ministry. A pastor should be involved and invested in the lives of the people they are shepherding. Effectively pastoring more that 20-30 people really isn't possible. All

---

[3] I have a training course on the fivefold ministry that I would love to offer to my readers free of charge. I have also produced a booklet on the fivefold ministry for those who prefer the written word. The link to both is https://timothyjemly.com/freebook

the other types of ministers, the teacher, the evangelist, the prophet, and the apostle, could serve large groups at once. So God in his wisdom gives more pastors than any other type of minister.

Next are teachers. Teachers can help people understand new concepts or ways of doing things. This includes teaching the Bible and showing individuals how to live Christ-centered lives. It is not limited to that, however. You can be a teacher who teaches math, surfing, or how to fix a bicycle, and if you do it as a servant while looking for ways to point people to God, you are ministering.

The third type of minister is an evangelist. When we hear the word 'evangelist' we often picture someone up on a stage preaching to thousands of people, and that is one way to do it. Most evangelists, however, talk with people one-on-one. Evangelists don't have to use pressure tactics or be pushy. Evangelists simply have the passion and ability to share with others what God can do for them.

The fourth type of minister is a prophet. This doesn't mean someone who foretells the future, although that could be a small part of what they do. A prophet is someone who hears God's Word for a specific situation and can share it with others. They are often very concerned with truth and with justice. They are good at seeing where there is injustice going on and call people to action to resolve the injustices they see in the world.

The fifth type of minister is an apostle. All of Jesus' disciples were apostles, so it is tempting to think this is some kind of special assignment. Apostles are all about starting new things and entering fresh territory for God. Jesus was starting His church, so that was what they needed at the time. An apostle is always trying to 'take the next hill' for God, they are always seeking new people and trying to start new ministries for God. They get excited about the next new thing. They need to have some good pastors surrounding them who will help them keep the territory they seized. Otherwise, when they conquer a new hill, they could be losing the one they conquered last.

In the fivefold ministry the apostles, evangelists and prophets are like the pioneers. They went out and explored unknown land and conquered fresh territory. Behind the pioneers would come the settlers who would build the roads, farms, hotels, all the infrastructure of society. The pastor and teachers are like the settlers who come in behind the apostles, prophets, and evangelists, and do the work necessary to maintain the territory that has been taken.

If God composed the church of only pastors and teachers, then everyone in the church would feel loved and cared for, but the church would never reach anyone new. If He had only given apostles, evangelists, and prophets then we would reach lots of new people but they would leave the church as soon as they came in because there would be nobody to shepherd them. We need each other to accomplish God's purposes.

Why the emphasis on ministry if we find our purpose by knowing God? The more we know Him and understand we are part of His body, the more we will recognize that we are ministers. The ministry we do flows out of our identity as part of the body of Christ. If we are going to thrive, we must root ourselves in Him **and** live out our role as ministers. Our hearts will always yearn for something more until we truly walk out this truth.

Chapter 10

Enter the Dance

There was a time in my life when I carried around a day planner and had literally every fifteen-minute block of my time planned out. I determined to squeeze as much productivity out of my time as possible. I hurried from one crisis to the next since things always seem to come up that I hadn't accounted for in my schedule. Worse, I felt stifled and joyless as I love being spontaneous and having variety in my day. I was trying to make someone else's system work for me, and it was crushing me. If I hadn't made a change, I probably would have ended up in the hospital with a nervous breakdown.

At another point in my journey, I started focusing on balance. I realized that if I was going to thrive, I needed to thrive in my career/finances, in my relationships, in my spirituality, and my health. The problem was, I couldn't seem to achieve the balance I was striving for. It seemed there was always an imbalance in one area that required more of my attention, and I would feel guilty and beat myself up for not keeping up with the all the things I knew I should be doing in the other areas. It was emotionally draining, completely depleting my energy levels.

I remember watching Nik Wallenda walk a high-wire across the Grand Canyon. It was stressful just watching him! The Holy Spirit spoke to me and said, "That's what balance looks like. Every muscle taught, always reacting to the tiniest change in the wind. It's stressful and progress is slow. Let me offer you another way—come and dance with me." In my mind's eye, I saw myself dancing with Jesus. There was so much joy and freedom in that picture that a longing to make that my daily reality grew in my heart.

When I think of all I want to accomplish in my relationships, health, spirituality, career, and making the world a better place to live, there's always more to do than I could hope to achieve. When I was striving for balance, there was always a sadness and a guilt that I hadn't done everything I know I should do if I want to make real progress in each of those areas. It seemed like I was running from thing to thing but never making genuine progress on any of my goals. However, when I embraced life as a dance with Jesus, things changed.

A few observations about dancing: First, if you want to dance, you have to learn the steps. Second, dancing is a chauvinistic endeavor—the man always leads. As Christ's bride, we are the followers in the dance. Third, you have to hear the music. Let's begin with learning the steps. There are basic steps to every dance that we must learn through discipline and practice. Once we learn those basic steps, however, there's an infinite variety of spins, tosses, twirls, and slides that we can layer on top of those basic moves. The follower in the dance need not worry about all the things that they could be doing. If we're in time with the music, if we're following our partner's lead, and using the basic steps then we're golden. Ecclesiastes 3:1 asserts,

> *"There is a time for everything, and a season for every activity under the heavens" (NIV)*

Entering the dance means learning to do the right thing at the right time. The freedom this brings is I no longer need to balance all the things I should do. I only need to know the right thing for this moment and do that. I am my most productive and joyful self when I am listening to the Spirit and doing what He leads me to do.

Consistently staying in this place of joy and fruitfulness requires the same three things as dancing. First, we must learn the basic steps. In life that equates to scheduling regular times of *up, in, out, and forward. Up* means time spent connecting to God, *In* refers to time spent with family and Christian friends, *Out* refers to time spent connecting with non-Christian friends and neighbors, and finally, *Forward* is the time we spend working on the projects and passions that God has placed in our heart.

It takes discipline and work to learn to make these four areas part of the regular patterns and rhythms of our daily life. It's hard work at first, but it's a lot less work than trying to balance by myself the dozens of things I know I need to be doing. I block out time for each of those four areas and then I ask Jesus to show me what He wants me to do in the area I have set aside this time for.

While dancing one may get away from the basic steps to accomplish a complex movement, but we always come back to them. In the same way, I may not always stick to the rhythms I have set up because they aren't rules, but a foundation that I build on. If I fail to return to that foundation my life will soon get out of control, but I have the freedom to move away from it as the Spirit leads me, which is the perfect segue into the second way the abundant life is like dancing. We must follow the lead of our partner.

When two people are dancing the leader communicates his intentions to his partner through very subtle movements. The more often two people dance, the easier it is for communication to happen. Most Christians have experienced God's leading at some point in their life. They can tell you how God closed or opened a door, how He whispered to their heart, how He provided a miraculous sign, or how He used another person to speak to them. However, getting that kind of direction on a moment-by-moment basis is foreign to many people.

Learning to listen constantly and respond to the subtle movements of God's Spirit could seem overwhelming. It doesn't have to be, however. Part of the magic in dancing is the foundation of the basic steps and the addition of certain basic moves. When you're dancing, it isn't necessary for the leader to communicate everything that the follower needs to do, but only what move they intend to go into next. When learning a new move, more communication and practice are necessary, but once it's learned, it only requires a gentle touch or nudge to move the follower into a very complicated movement. It's the same way in our lives. When we block out time for the four basic rhythms of our lives, *up, in, out, and forward*, and we allow God to teach us what He wants us to do in each area, we learn repeatable patterns that only require His gentle nudge to move us into.

Let me give a practical example to help clarify what I'm talking about. I set aside time each week to bless my neighbors. It is part of the regular rhythm of "*out*" that I block into my schedule. As I pray for my neighbors and ask God what He wants for me to do, a thought may come to mind that I haven't seen my elderly neighbor Dorothy in a while. That could be God nudging me to bring her some dessert and sit and talk awhile.

On the other hand, if I simply wake up in the morning and ask God, "What do you want me to do today?" it is a lot harder for Him to just nudge me in a certain direction because the three hundred to-dos on **my** list come rushing at me. Don't misunderstand me, I think asking God first thing in the morning what He wants us to do is a great habit. I often practice this discipline, but it takes a lot more communication and work for me to get a clear message on what God is saying. If I'm wanting His direction on a moment-by-moment basis, it is very helpful to have the "steps" already choreographed so that all it takes is a gentle touch to move me in the right direction.

The third ingredient in good dancing is listening to the music. Listening to the music does three things. First, it informs us what type of dance we're doing. If the music is a waltz and I'm trying to do the basic steps for the tango things will not go so well-- especially if my partner is doing the waltz! Second, music inspires us to get up and actually dance—it brings the spark and the joy that makes us want to move. Third, music helps my partner and I to move together.

How does this apply to our lives? I believe each of us has a life song that inspires us to act, and helps us to move in unison with God, and that teaches us the basic steps we need to do to fulfill our unique purpose. How do we hear and recognize this song? There are five elements that make up any piece of music, and the music of our lives is composed of five aspects that correspond with these elements. The five ingredients of music are: melody, harmony, key, meter, and rhythm. In the music of our lives, our emotions perform the melody. Emotions give texture and richness to our lives. Without them, our lives would be bland and colorless. Our relationships bring harmony to our lives. They enhance our positive emotions and bring a sympathetic richness to our sadness. The key the music is written in tells you which notes can be included in the song, and just as importantly, which notes to exclude.

Back in the chapter on emotions, I wrote about the need to rid our lives of fear, bitterness, and resentment because those emotions are off-key in the song God has composed for our lives. Meter refers to the way a song is counted, how we use our time. Rhythm is the rests and beats that give the song movement. In my life song, this is the interplay between rest and work that make up the warp and woof of our daily lives.

God wrote the music of our lives to inspire us to dance—to do things He created us for. But how does that happen in practicality? At the heart of any song is the melody, which corresponds to our emotions. It took me a long time to figure it out, but my emotions were actually the missing key to getting every area of life synergistically coming together. At one time, emotional health wasn't part of my definition of thriving. In fact, I discounted the importance of emotions. I would tell people to ignore their emotions and decide based on the Word of God and sound logic. I said this because I have seen so many people make a mess of their lives by making unwise decisions based on their emotions. I still maintain that we shouldn't allow emotions color important decisions, however, I now understand that my emotions are an important part of my overall well-being. If my emotional life gets out of whack, it will negatively influence my health, my ability to get things done, and even my spiritual life.

I now consider emotional and spiritual well-being to be the twin lynchpins on which we base the abundant life. Emotions give us the passion, desire and energy to accomplish the tasks necessary for thriving in every other area of life. It is the melody of the song that drives us, while spirituality gives us the wisdom to know what do and the God-given skills to do it. Our thoughts, emotions, and connection to God comprise the internal reality of our lives. If we thrive in these areas, it will eventually translate to the outer parts of our lives. If our internal reality is chaotic, it will inevitably cause our external world to fall apart.

An example of this is procrastination. When we have decided that something is important and worthy of our time but we keep putting it off, it is a sign of an internal disconnect. We blame our circumstances—I'm just too busy-- but that isn't the real problem. For most of my life, I have been a procrastinator because I couldn't seem to muster the energy and focus needed to finish an assignment without a looming deadline. It took me a long time to realize that this was actually an emotional problem. I was relying on the anxiety and stress to push me into activity instead of allowing my desires and passion to stir me into action. Consider the results of this lifestyle. First, stress is terrible for our health. Second, we might convince ourselves otherwise, but we can't really perform at our best under constant stress. Third, there is no possible way to thrive in every area of our life because we are constantly ignoring the areas which aren't currently in crisis. If we only put effort in when there is a crises we may find we've waited too long when the crisis strikes our important relationships or our spirituality.

So how do we break free of the procrastination trap? Proverbs 13:4 says,

> "*The soul of a lazy man desires, and has nothing; But the soul of the diligent shall be made rich.*" *(NKJV)*

The problem with laziness, according to this verse, is a lack of desire! I read that and thought that can't be right, I have powerful desires! However, I realized that while I didn't lack passion for the things I needed to do, I wasn't accessing my desires when I needed them. This revelation along with the realization that I can control my emotions has allowed me finally to break the lifelong habit of procrastinating.

I began this chapter by describing the time in my life when I had every 15 minutes of my week planned out. This was my attempt to overcome procrastination with discipline and focus. It failed miserably. I no longer use a regimented time management system, but I do block out major sections of time for *up, in, out and forward*. Instead, I concentrate on managing my energy and my emotions. Most of us waste a lot of time and don't work nearly as efficiently as we are capable of. Often, we don't have energy when we need it. Other times we have energy but we don't feel like tackling our most important projects so we engage in less important tasks so we can feel good that we've gotten something done.

So, how have I learned to control my emotions and manage my energy levels? These two things are very interconnected because our emotions affect our energy levels and our energy levels affect our emotions. Therefore, it's important to work both halves at the same time. Some people are skeptical when I tell them I can control my emotions. They have this idea that emotions just happen and there is nothing you or I do to change them. The truth is, there is a cause for every emotion, and if I change the cause I change the emotion. I am a very emotional guy; I admit to often crying at movies. I can usually see it coming though, there is this buildup that happens. If I don't want to get emotional, I could leave the theater and buy popcorn or change the channel and watch Duck Dynasty. The principle I want to make clear is if we change our focus, we change our emotions. We can choose what to focus both our physical and mental eyes on, therefore we can choose our emotions.

I am not advocating that we put our heads in the sand and ignore reality. If a loved one dies, we don't just look at rainbows and think happy thoughts. We need to allow ourselves to experience the painful emotions when they are appropriate. Ecclesiastes 3 says there is a season for everything and it lists weeping and morning as part of a litany of things that there is a proper time for. What I am saying is that when we know what the appropriate thing for a given moment is, we need to access the emotions that will propel us into action—the music that inspires us to dance.

Let's use diet and exercise as another example. If I decide to change my diet radically and start exercising more, I am going to need some powerful motivators to keep me going. So, I would begin by doing a mental exercise where I ask myself why a new diet and exercise is important. I don't stop with the surface level though. I am going to go seven layers deep asking why my reason is important. For instance, let's say I decided my first reason is "*I want to look good.*" I would then ask why that is important. To which I might answer, "*I want my wife to be attracted to me*". Now, I am two layers deep, but I need to go seven. It probably won't take all seven layers for me to realize that this reason is actually based on fear and pride.

Fear of not being accepted, or being good enough, and pride in wanting others to admire me. Those things are off key for my life song, so I would have to find a better reason.

The second, first level, reason I might consider for the exercise and diet changes is, "*I want to be healthy.*" Again, I am going to take this seven layers deep. By the time I get to the seventh layer I might end up saying, "I want to be able to inspire my grandkids to seek the abundant life Jesus offers as I play sports with them." Now, when I don't feel like going to the gym, I am going to imagine my future grandkid being with me in heaven and them telling me they are there because I took the time to play baseball with them every week and talk with them about Jesus. If I have truly discovered my deepest why, then imaging that scene will cause a strong emotional response that will push me to go the gym because I want to be healthy enough to make that a reality.

We can manage our emotions by using visualization and focusing our eyes on the things that will unlock the emotions we need to thrive. How do we manage our energy though?

The creation story told in Genesis says that the evening and the morning made up each day. It always lists the evening first. Evenings are for rest and restoration, daytime is for work and productivity. So in God's way of doing things, we rest first and then we work from our rest. God created Adam and Eve on the sixth day of the week, the next day was the Sabbath—a day of rest. Before they had ever done anything, God gave them a full day of rest. God designed that we would always work from the overflow, never allowing ourselves to become depleted. Most people work until they're exhausted and then rest. We desperately need to learn God's rhythms for life. One of my favorite authors said it this way,

"As an aspiring musician, rhythm is my Achilles heel. People that don't know me very well will say silly things like 'You've just got to feel it.' People that know me well don't say that, instead they show me where I am going wrong and how it's supposed to go. The problem is that I feel the music really well. I really get into it. But then I sometimes get so into it I just can't wait to start the next phrase, and I come in a count or two early. Other times I am feeling it so much that I just want to hold that note out, or add a little 'shoo, wop, bop'. Which, of course, adds extra beats to the song. It works fine when I am the only one singing but when I am playing with others and they don't all feel the same thing I do, it doesn't work. I find that it really helps when I am playing with a strong drummer who can emphasize the downbeats. It is like being able to hear the heartbeat of the music. I believe that many people live lives of chaos and stress because they fail to hear the steady heartbeat of God."[xiv]

What I described in that passage is the meter of the music. Our rhythm will always be in chaos if we don't understand the meter—how we count the music. In the song of our life, the meter is how we count our time. The earth rotating on its axis measures off a day. The moon rotating around the earth loosely measures off our month. The year comes from the rotation of the earth around the sun. Where does the weekly cycle come from? It is the meter for the music of the spheres. Six days of work followed by one day of rest. If our lives are not in sync with this rhythm, we will constantly fall back into striving instead of resting in Christ and allowing His grace to do the work.

When I talk about the Sabbath people always seem to get nervous and think I am advocating for legalism. The reality is just the opposite. One of the central themes of this book is that all of God's laws are descriptive, not arbitrary. If we live our lives in alignment with those laws we're blessed, if we are out of alignment, bad things happen. We are incapable of living fully in alignment with these laws in our strength. However, because of the sacrifice of Jesus, we're given the grace to keep the law and reap the blessings. God places us in Christ and He lives in us. He lives His perfect life through us and we reap the rewards. This is the essence of the abundant life.

Hebrews 4:9-11 makes this progression clear. It says,

"There remains, then, a Sabbath-rest for the people of God; for anyone who enters God's rest also rests from their works, just as God did from his. Let us, therefore, make every effort to enter that rest, so that no one will perish by following their example of disobedience." (NIV)

God's rest is something that we enter; it isn't just a ceasing from our own work. Jesus is our rest and we must enter into Him. When we enter His rest, we will also rest from our works. Why? Because He lives in us and therefore, we will follow His patterns and rhythms. This isn't about salvation, but it's about the abundant life. We're saved the moment we accept Jesus as our Lord and Savior. But if we want to enjoy the abundant life, we must learn to let Him transform all of our daily habits and routines.

This is the last piece of the music. The Sabbath acts as a tutor to teach us how to enter God's rest. It is a weekly reminder not to depend on ourselves for our provision, but to trust God to take care of us. When we stray into anxiety, striving, and selfish ambition, a Sabbath rest is a weekly pause point to get us back on track. If we get out of step with God, it's the strong downbeat in the music enabling us to get back in sync. It is a constant reminder that we can't thrive on our own power; we need the grace of God to carry us.

We have really come full circle. We began this journey talking about the grace of God and its miraculous power to transform us, and that is also where we will end. God is calling us to enter the dance, to live with abandon and joy, and we can only do this through His grace. Are you ready to step forward, take God's hand and be His dance partner?

I hope you enjoyed this book and that it has been a blessing in your life. Please consider leaving me a review on Amazon or Goodreads to help others discover this book as well.

About the Author

Timothy Jemly is the author of the Amazon best-selling book <u>God's Submarines</u>, and his newest book which you currently hold in your hands along with its companion book <u>Unlock Your Purpose.</u> Besides being a writer, Timothy is also pastor and church planter with a passion for helping people cultivate a deeper relationship with God. During his senior year in high school, his mother passed away, leaving him broken and hungry for deep relationships. He turned to God to fill that need and found out the tools he'd been taught for connecting with God were insufficient for the depth he desired. During this tough season of life, he began reflecting on what Jesus meant by the abundant life He promised to those who follow Him.

What started as his personal desire to know God better and discover the secrets to true abundance has turned into a lifelong quest to share with others the things he learned.

He has taught thousands of people the blueprint he ultimately discovered for developing intimacy with God and allowing Him to transform every area of life.

Timothy currently pastors Coastal Christian Fellowship in Jacksonville Beach, Florida, which he planted in 2018. He enjoys dating his beautiful wife, engaging with his daughter, playing board games, climbing, surfing and kayaking.

Want to learn more from Timothy Jemly?

Follow me on Facebook

facebook.com/TimothyJemlyAuthor/

Signup for my newsletter and get a free ecopy of Unlock Your Purpose visit https://timothyjemly.com/freebook

Check out my first book God's Submarines on Amazon.

Endnotes

i - CHRISTINE CARTER, PH.D. IN PSYCHOLOGY TODAY

HTTPS://WWW.PSYCHOLOGYTODAY.COM/US/BLOG/RAISING-

HAPPINESS/201412/WHY-HAPPINESS-IS-THE-WRONG-PURSUIT-0

ii HTTPS://WWW.NYTIMES.COM/2015/01/09/STYLE/NO-37-BIG-WEDDING-OR-SMALL.HTML

iii HTTPS://ARCHIVE.ORG/DETAILS/BODILYCHANGESINP00CANN/MODE/2UP

iv KAPLAN R. "THE PSYCHOLOGICAL BENEFITS OF NEARBY NATURE." IN D.

RELF (ED.) THE ROLE OF HORTICULTURE IN HUMAN WELL BEING AND SOCIAL

DEVELOPMENT: A NATIONAL SYMPOSIUM. PORTLAND, OR: TIMBER PRESS.

1992: 128, 130.

v ULRICH R, SIMONS R ET AL. "STRESS RECOVERY DURING EXPOSURE TO

NATURAL AND URBAN ENVIRONMENTS." JOURNAL OF ENVIRONMENTAL

PSYCHOLOGY 1991 11: 201-230.

vi LEATHER P, PYGRAS M, BEALE D, LAWRENCE C "WINDOWS IN THE

WORKPLACE: SUNLIGHT, VIEW, AND OCCUPATIONAL STRESS." ENVIRONMENT

AND BEHAVIOR, 1998, 30:739-762.

vii Roach, Mary Packing for Mars: The Curious Science of Life in the Void.

viii https://www.dosseydossey.com/larry/book.html

ix Ornish D. Love and Survival: The Scientific Basis for the Healing Power of Intimacy. New York: HarperCollins, 1998, 2-3.

x Padus E. The Complete guide to Your Emotions and Your Health: New Dimensions in Mind/ Body Healing. Emmaus, Penn.: Rodale Press, 1986, 648.

xi Egolf, B; Lasker, J; Wolf, S; Potvin, L (1992). "The Roseto Effect: A 50-Year Comparison of Mortality Rates". American Journal of Public Health. 82 (8): 1089–1092. DOI:10.2105/AJPH.82.8.1089. PMC 1695733. PMID 1636828.

xii https://time.com/4176128/powerball-jackpot-lottery-winners/
xiii Available on Amazon at this link:

https://www.amazon.com/dp/B082GQDVF2

xiv Timothy Jemly, God's Submarines p. 123

Made in the USA
Columbia, SC
19 July 2021